Bread of Life

Exploring the Presence
of Eucharist
in Our Lives

Louis J. Cameli

LITURGY
TRAINING
PUBLICATIONS

Nihil Obstat
Very Reverend Daniel A. Smilanic, JCD
Vicar for Canonical Services
Archdiocese of Chicago
December 29, 2011

Imprimatur
Reverend John F. Canary, STL, DMIN
Vicar General
Archdiocese of Chicago
December 29, 2011

The *Nihil Obstat* and *Imprimatur* are official declarations that the material is free from doctrinal or moral error, and thus is granted permission to publish in accordance with c. 827. No legal responsibility is assumed by the grant of this permission. No implication is contained herein that those who have granted the *Nihil Obstat* and *Imprimatur* agree with the content, opinions, or statements expressed.

Library of Congress Control Number: 2012934073

16 15 14 13 12   1 2 3 4 5

ISBN 978-1-61671-058-3

BOL

Contents

Foreword

The most moving experiences of my ministry as Archbishop of Chicago are celebrating Mass with people of the Archdiocese at Holy Name Cathedral and in the parishes. When we are gathered to hear God's Word and to share in the Bread of Life, when we enter into the mystery of the Lord's self-sacrificing love present in the Mass, when in Holy Communion we become one with him who became one with us, we are most truly ourselves.

The Eucharist shapes and transforms us as disciples of Jesus Christ. The Eucharist enables us to become more and more "sons and daughters of God in the Son, Jesus Christ," in the words of theologian Emile Meersch.

As the Archdiocese of Chicago embarks with the Church Universal on a Year of Faith in 2012, proclaimed by Pope Benedict XVI with a special focus on our celebration of the Mystery of Faith in the Eucharist, I am confident that Father Louis Cameli's book will be a valuable resource. Father Cameli has brought his own faith, his erudition and his clarity of thought to this work, and all of us are the richer.

God gives us this graced time to rediscover the mysteries of faith and to rediscover our deepest identity in Jesus Christ. The Eucharist, which is "the source and summit of the Christian life," can lead, guide, and direct us to this double rediscovery and give us strength to follow Christ joyfully.

The demands of daily life, the barrage of messages that flood our lives, the uncertain directions of this world—all these pull us in many different directions. We may seldom or never feel centered or at peace or, for that matter, really ourselves. In faith, we can reclaim our true center in God and begin to sort out what truly matters.

In the Eucharist and in our encounter with the living Christ, we will find that true center. All that is required of us is attention, alertness, and a ready generosity.

May the reflections of this book and, even more, our shared journey in this Year of Faith and Year of the Eucharist lead us forward to Christ, the Bread of Life, the Bread of Hope.

Francis Cardinal George, OMI
Archbishop of Chicago

Part One

Chapter 1

Introduction:
Eucharist as Question

I cannot imagine my life without the Eucharist. A little later, as I share my eucharistic autobiography, you may better understand why the Eucharist means so much to me. My whole life has been intertwined with this great sacrament.

As a priest, I am also very much aware that not everyone values the Eucharist as I do, even many who claim to belong to the household of faith. As long as I have been a priest—and that covers the past forty-two years—parents and grandparents have frequently approached me in distress about their children or grandchildren. "Father, tell my kids to go to Mass," they might say. Or, they would ask me, "What can I tell my grandkids to get them to go to Mass?" I understand the urgency of their request. They know that the ones they love most, by their absence from the Eucharist, are denying themselves the essential spiritual sustenance which is the Lord himself.

Inside their words, I hear their assumption or perhaps their hope that I may have the magic and convincing formula that could move their children and grandchildren to regular participation in the Mass. I don't have a quick and convincing formula to offer them. Rather, I suggest another path. I encourage them to share with their children and grandchildren why the Mass, why Christ present in the Eucharist has meant so much to them. I invite them to give witness to the importance of the Eucharist in their lives and how the Eucharist has been both a sustaining and transforming power for them. What their children and grandchildren need to hear is how important the Eucharist is in the lives of people who matter to them. They need to know in personal ways that the Eucharist is truly the Bread of Life, that without it, we perish.

> From the very beginning of the Church and into our own day, the Eucharist has always triggered questions. Each age and culture has had its own particular questions. Our question—*Is the Eucharist that important?*

I am completely convinced that the fundamental question about the Eucharist today is this: *Is the Eucharist that important?* In the United States, large numbers of Catholics have answered that question in the negative. In effect, they say, "No, it's not that important." When, for example, in my own diocese only 23 percent of the Catholic population consistently participates in the Sunday Eucharist, the vast majority are saying with their absence, "Maybe the Eucharist is important, but it's not *that* important. Maybe the Eucharist is important at First Holy Communion, especially as a rite of passage. Or, it may be important at a wedding or funeral or even for the two major Christian celebrations of the year—Christmas and Easter. It is not so important, however, that it needs to be at the center of my life and wound into the narrative of my whole existence. It is certainly not so important that it needs to be prioritized and integrated into the basic rhythm of my life."

Is the Eucharist that important? This is the eucharistic question of our time. The question belongs particularly to us in North America and Europe at the beginning of the twenty-first century. And as I raise this eucharistic question of our time, be aware that questions about the Eucharist are not new. From the very beginning of the Church and into our own day, the Eucharist has always triggered questions. Each age and culture has had its own particular questions. Our question—*Is the Eucharist that important?*— belongs to that history of questions, but in its precise formulation, it is also unprecedented. Permit me to share a little history of questions surrounding the Eucharist and then to return to our current situation and its deeply challenging question about the Eucharist.

Questions concerning the Eucharist belong to the earliest history of the Church. For example, Paul spoke to the Church in Corinth and affirmed the unity signified and effected by the Eucharist. As he did so, he raised a question: *"The bread that we break, is it not a sharing in the body of Christ? Because there is one bread, we who are many are one body, for we all partake of the one bread"* (1 Corinthians 10:16b–17). And shortly thereafter, he raises more questions, now about the eucharistic inconsistency of an assembly that celebrates its oneness in Christ and then divides itself in the very act of celebration: *"Now in the following instructions I do not commend you, because when you come together it is not for the better but for the worse. For, to begin with, when you come together as a church, I hear that there are divisions among you. . . . When you come together, it is not really to eat the Lord's supper. For when the time comes to eat, each of you goes ahead with your own supper, and one goes hungry and another becomes drunk"* (1 Corinthians 11:17–18, 20–21).

Later, in the early centuries of the Church, the Fathers of the Church offered spiritually insightful teachings concerning the Eucharist. And these teachings were in response to questions about how the Eucharist sustains our spiritual lives. Listen, for example to these words of Saint Ephrem in the fourth century: "In your sacrament we daily embrace you and receive you into our bodies; make us worthy to experience the resurrection for which we hope. We have had your treasure hidden within us ever since we received baptismal grace; it grows ever richer at your sacramental table."[1]

A new set of challenges and concerns arose with the incorporation of the Frankish and Germanic peoples into the Church. These were the so-called "barbarians" whom many of us can count as our ancestors. The new converts brought their traditional attachment to physical markers and relics into their new Christian faith. And so, quite naturally the Eucharist fell under the sway of that attachment to tangible signs. Questions arose about the Eucharist as an object, as laden with power, and as a source of miracles.[2]

With the Middle Ages and later during the Reformation, questions about the Eucharist shifted again. There was great concern about the exact nature of Christ's presence in the Eucharist and many questions about how exactly the bread and wine became the Body and Blood of the Lord. Responding to proposals of the Protestant reformers, the Council of Trent clearly taught that the substance of bread and wine became the substance of the Body and Blood of the Lord, a process of change that the Church ". . . has fittingly and properly called transubstantiation."[3]

Now we can return to our own time. Some of the older questions persist. For example, some people ask about miracles associated with the Eucharist and some others ask about alternate theological formulations to capture the change in the elements of bread and wine. As we already noted, however, today's major question about the Eucharist has to do with its significance: *Is the Eucharist really that important?* The precipitous decline of participation in the Eucharist in North America and Europe suggests that many who self-identify as Catholics are deeply shaped by our surrounding secular and skeptical culture.[4] And that secular formation has led to a greatly diminished sense of the power and meaning of the Eucharist.

When so many people who might claim a Catholic identity absent themselves from the Eucharist, they manifest either an utterly deficient understanding of this sacrament or such a low regard for it that they readily allow other priorities to displace their participation in the Eucharist. In either case, whether it is a matter of understanding or of value or perhaps a combination of both, the situation is very serious.

The question—*Is the Eucharist that important?*—is historically unprecedented in our family of faith. In the past, even if people did not fully understand the value of the Eucharist or did not live up to the priority of the Eucharist, they would have certainly acknowledged that the Eucharist was very important, at least in theory. In contrast, today people seem ready to excuse themselves from participating in the Mass, because the Eucharist does not seem to be *that* important even in a general, notional way. As one woman once said to me, "You can't be serious that it's a grave sin to miss Mass on Sunday." Her statement assumes, as she explained it, that you cannot have "grave matter" for something that is "just a strong recommendation." This nonchalant attitude regarding the Eucharist is deeply troubling and even alarming.

According to the Second Vatican Council, the Eucharist is "the source and summit of the Christian life."[5] The Eucharist is at the very center of faith. A light, sporadic, casual, or only occasional participation signals that something is very, very wrong.

We began with the concerns of parents and grandparents about their kids and grandkids not going to Mass on Sunday. We can see that their concerns are well placed. Faith is deeply diminished when people, by their absence, can assert that the Eucharist is not *that* important.

In the pages of this book, I want to say, "No. The Eucharist is, indeed, *that* important. It is at the center of our faith." "For in the most blessed Eucharist is contained the whole spiritual good of the Church, namely Christ himself our Pasch and the living bread which gives life. . . ."[6]

Affirming and explaining the importance and centrality of the Eucharist can take shape in various approaches or methods. I will follow an approach guided by three questions. Recall the overarching contemporary question: *Is the Eucharist that important?* To respond to it, I will begin with the recommendation that I offer to parents and grandparents who are dealing with their children who do not go to Mass or do not do so regularly. As I noted earlier, I tell those parents to tell their children what the Eucharist means for them, how it has been so important for them, and why it is essential in their life of faith. Personal witness to the significance of the Eucharist is a decisive moment of communication.

I will pick up the first question, which is a deeply personal question, and try to answer it personally: *How has the Eucharist been central to my journey of faith?* To answer this question—not theoretically but personally—I want to share with you what I call my *eucharistic autobiography.* I will share the story of my life and how the Eucharist has been woven into my life overall, connected with the movement of my human development, and linked to my unfolding journey of faith. I share this eucharistic story of my life not because it sets a pattern for others or because it is extraordinary. My life is quite ordinary, and I would never claim that it is normative for others. I share this story as an invitation extended to you to gather the elements of your own eucharistic story. If as individual believers and as a Church we are to give witness to the power and centrality of the Eucharist, then we must be conscious and clear about that power and centrality in our own lives. We need to take hold of our eucharistic experience, find the right language to express it, and then generously and unself-consciously share that with others. In brief, I want my eucharistic autobiography to trigger your process of gathering and articulating your own eucharistic autobiography. I am completely convinced that there is unparalleled power to evangelize and re-evangelize when we speak from the heart about God's mercy and gift manifested in our experience of the Eucharist. That is the import of the eucharistic autobiography.

> **The lingering general question is: *Is the Eucharist that important?* And the first step of responding to that question is another question: *How is the Eucharist important to me?* Answering that question means articulating our eucharistic autobiography.**

The lingering general question is: *Is the Eucharist that important?* And the first step of responding to that question is another question: *How is the Eucharist important to me?* Answering that question means articulating our eucharistic autobiography. The second step in response to the question of the importance of the Eucharist is a turn to the Word of God, and bringing a second question to the Sacred Scriptures: *What did Jesus want to give us when he gave us the Eucharist?* As we discover the intention of Jesus in giving himself to us in the Eucharist, we also uncover in a new and unparalleled way the importance of the Eucharist.

The Gospel offers us many passages for considering the intention of Jesus with regard to the Eucharist. I will focus on one chapter of John's account of the Gospel, chapter six, and the "Bread of Life Discourse." In this chapter and in a concentrated way, Jesus speaks of himself as the Bread of Life. The chapter moves us deeper and deeper into the mind of Jesus through a series of fourteen questions raised by Jesus, his disciples, and others. From the one who gives us the Eucharist, from the one who *is* the Eucharist, we grasp its centrality and importance. In yet another way, through a *lectio divina,* or holy and meditative reading of chapter six of John's account of the Gospel, we find answers to that question that frames our horizon: *Is the Eucharist that important?*

Finally, a third step picks up the question of the significance of the Eucharist by correlating important human and spiritual experience with the Eucharist. Here the specific question is: *How can we link important elements of human and spiritual experience with the Eucharist?* In effect, this is another way of asking, "What does the Eucharist mean in our lives, especially in important aspects of our lives?" Here, we will consider the Eucharist and the question of life and death, the question of human sexuality, the question of God's immanence and transcendence, the question of violence and reconciliation, the question of transformation, the question of the moral measure of our lives, the question of our mission and purpose, the question of our fragility, and the question of our future.

Humanly and spiritually, these questions are of the utmost importance. If the Eucharist illumines and responds to these questions, we can be assured of the importance of the Eucharist and its enduring power to address the most significant and often perplexing questions generated by our human condition and our spiritual journey.

At the end of our reflections, we shall have responded to the one overarching question: *Is the Eucharist that important?* Our response will be deeply personal, because it will emerge in a eucharistic autobiography from the very narrative of our existence. It will be an entirely assured response, because it will be spoken from the words of Jesus and the experience of the earliest Christian communities as chapter six of John's account of the Gospel gives witness to that experience. Finally, our response will be a genuine and real response, because it will not shrink from the difficult and challenging dimensions of human experience that mark all our lives and on which we will reflect with the help of theology.

Questions for Reflection and Sharing

After each major section of this book, questions for personal reflection and group sharing are offered. The questions are meant to help you personalize the contents of the chapters. If you have the opportunity after your personal reflection to share with others who have also reflected on the chapters, this will enrich and expand your own understanding. We begin with two questions for reflection and sharing after the introduction.

1.   Do you think that there are reasons to be concerned about how the Eucharist is understood, valued, and celebrated today?

2.   In your life experience, do you sense a shift among Catholics concerning their attitude toward the Eucharist and their participation in the Eucharist?

Chapter 2

My Eucharistic Autobiography

As I offer my eucharistic autobiography, recall its purpose. I share my eucharistic autobiography as an invitation to others to retrieve and articulate their own eucharistic autobiographies. When we identify the transforming power of the Eucharist in the course of our lives, we are then able to give witness to the significance and meaning of this sacrament. Our experience can serve as an invitation to others to claim the importance of the Eucharist.

The guiding question for my eucharistic autobiography has been: *How has the Eucharist been central to my journey of faith?* Raise this question for yourself. Ponder it. Allow memories to surface. Seek to understand particular experiences as well as practices, stretched over longer periods of time. This is what I tried to do, and this is what I share with you.

Earliest Memories

I cannot pinpoint the exact time, but I must have been three and a half years old or maybe closer to four. I was brought to San Rocco Church early in the morning. I do not remember who brought me, but we went into a pew about three-quarters of the way to the back of the church, reflecting the usual gravitational pull of Catholics to the back of the church. I stood on the kneeler but could barely see the altar up front. It was brightly lit and crowded with colorful statues. The place smelled funny too—now I know it was the smell of burning wax. Whoever took me to church tried to calm me down, told me to be quiet, and pointed to the altar and said, "God's up there." That did make me quiet, at least for a while, and left an impression on me, because I still remember it. I did not yet know the word *mystery*, but I met it that day. This was the beginning of my contact with the Eucharist. And it started from the back of church as I strained to get a glimpse of God on the altar surrounded by bright lights and colorful statues.

When I was four going on five, a few months after my grandfather had died, I went to San Rocco again. This time I was with my grandmother and in the company of a group of women from the neighborhood. They were all dressed in black and had black scarves on their heads. Later, much later, I knew they were dressed this way because they were all widows. And we all walked together along railroad tracks that ran behind my grandmother's house through a prairie where you could smell the wet grass in the very early summer morning when it was still half dark. We walked for about a mile to get to the church. While we walked, the women prayed the Rosary in a persistent low chant. Later, much later, the scene flashed in my mind's eye, and it looked like something from an Italian neo-realist film of the late 1940s. And, in fact, it was very much like that. We processed in sadness, because the Mass was for my grandfather who had died not so long before.

We came to the church, and the Mass began. The priest wore black. We prayed for my grandfather. And in that Mass I knew some connection with him, across the boundary of death. Here at Mass there was memory and presence, just like the lit candle that my grandmother kept in her bedroom to remember her husband. In ways I could not explain at that time, I knew that we could bring our sadness and our loss to the Mass and it would be held on that altar up front in the church.

First Holy Communion and Early Learning

The Franciscan Sisters of Perpetual Adoration of Mishawaka, Indiana taught at Saint Agnes School. Their "perpetual adoration" was adoration of the Eucharist. Not surprisingly, they prepared us for our First Holy Communion with great intensity and total determination. Sixty years later, I still remember the message and the drills. The message was simple and overwhelming: we would be receiving Jesus within ourselves, Jesus the Son of God, the Savior of the World, the King of the Universe. It was the starkest and most dramatic encounter of our lives. We were going to meet God who was coming to meet us intimately. I came to know the Eucharist as the transcendent mystery of God encountering finite human beings—and all this happening in the "ordinary form" of what looked like regular bread cut into a thin circle. Only many years later would I catch up with the language of mystery and gain some partial theological understanding of what I already knew in a very direct way when I was eight years old.

> I came to know the Eucharist as the transcendent mystery of God encountering finite human beings—and all this happening in the "ordinary form" of what looked like regular bread cut into a thin circle. Only many years later would I catch up with the language of mystery and gain some partial theological understanding of what I already knew in a very direct way when I was eight years old.

And then there were the drills in preparation for the day of First Holy Communion. We memorized prayers that we would recite together. Over and over again, we practiced saying them together. We also practiced our movements at Mass—our procession into the church, our going to the altar in neat groups to receive Holy Communion, and our procession out of the church at the end of Mass. All this we repeated under sharp and demanding eyes that would make Marine drill masters look utterly indolent. I went through the repetitions, of course, but felt desperately bored and impatient. Through it all, however, I did learn something important.

Our encounter with the Eucharist, if it is to mean something, is far from routine and certainly not casual. Jesus, I learned, makes himself available in the sacrament, but unless I have some disciplined attention and readiness, I can miss him. From that point on, I could not take Holy Communion for granted. It was not just a nice gesture. It meant heaven meeting earth, and I was in the middle.

The day of my First Holy Communion came, and it was extraordinary. Everything moved smoothly in church, and there was a great party afterward. It took a while to absorb what had happened. There was more to know and more to experience, and I was very interested to pursue both knowledge and experience of the Eucharist. An incredible and amazingly memorable classroom encounter in third grade brought me to another level of knowledge.

On a warm afternoon in 1953, Father Bill came to our third grade classroom "to teach us religion," they said. Later I found out that Father Bill had a doctorate in theology from a university in Rome. Passionately and systematically he unleashed his theological learning on our third-grade class that afternoon. And I have never forgotten the experience.

The women in the parish said that Father Bill was a handsome man. He dressed in a distinctive way. He always had a neatly folded white handkerchief in the breast pocket of his black suit coat. The afternoon he came to our class, however, he was wearing a cassock. He began his lesson with the story of the Israelites leaving Egypt and wandering in the desert. They were hungry, and they complained to Moses who prayed to God for them (see Exodus 16). In response to Moses' prayer, God sent them "manna"—bread from heaven. Then Father Bill jumped—and almost literally did this with crisscross diagrams on the blackboard—to the New Testament and chapter six of John's account of the Gospel, the Bread of Life discourse. Jesus, he said, was the true Bread that came down from heaven. And for us, this was the Eucharist given to us, today in the Mass and in Holy Communion. In that teaching, in some initial way, I came to understand that the Eucharist that is Jesus, our Bread of

Life, represents God's fidelity to us as we cross the desert and, even more, it represents the only thing that can truly sustain us.

This was one of a handful of remarkable "religion lessons" that I experienced as a child, but it was also sad in the context of Father Bill's life overall. He became an alcoholic. Eventually, he left town and the priesthood and married a local woman who was a doctor. They settled in Mexico where he became an English radio station announcer. In the end, he divorced and died in isolation, almost like the whiskey priest in Graham Greene's novel *The Power and the Glory*. I pray for him and trust that God's mercy has embraced him. He was God's instrument for me to come to know the Eucharist more deeply. He was a flawed and limited instrument, as we all are, and yet he was still an instrument. And my reflections on his life have taught me that even with knowledge of the ways of God in the Eucharist, we all have a fragile hold on holy things. We go forward tentatively, until we arrive at home.

The early years of elementary school brought me to another kind of eucharistic encounter. Our pastor was Monsignor Walter E. Croarkin. He had thoroughly absorbed a spirit that had taken hold of the Church in Chicago in the first half of the twentieth century, a progressive spirit that fostered active participation in the liturgy and linked that participation with a strong commitment to social justice. So, in these early school years we were each handed a little pamphlet that had all the responses of the Mass in Latin, of course. Once a week, on Wednesdays we had a *Missa recitata*, literally a "recited Mass." All the children in the school made all the responses that normally only the altar boys would make. This happened in the early 1950s, and it left its mark on me. I began to understand at a young age that I was not a spectator at Mass, that I was part of the Mass, and that I was a part of the Mass with all the others who prayed in unison. Years later I understood that these were practical foundations for what was the authentic renewal of the liturgy—full and active participation in community.

Serving Mass

Sixth grade was and is a tough time. It is the beginning of adolescence and with that, it is a time of new and awkward self-consciousness. It means beginning to compete with others to make a mark athletically, academically, and socially. At Saint Agnes School, sixth grade was the time when students could become altar boys. I jumped at the chance, and I am not quite sure why. Some of the reason surely had to do with my earlier experiences of the Eucharist, but no doubt a lot had to do with doing what boys were supposed to do in a Catholic school. As I prepared for serving, I was caught up in all the details, especially memorizing the Latin responses and learning the detailed movements that went into serving Mass. I took it on, I remember, not as a burden but as a challenge. I was determined to reach this milestone.

When all the preparing was completed and we were ready to begin serving Mass, I ran into a little roadblock. The priest in charge of altar boys—whom I later knew to be a very troubled person—gave precedence in scheduling to the three boys in my class whose fathers were doctors. At eleven years of age, I knew what was going on. I did not like it, but I was undeterred. I really wanted to serve Mass, and I would bide my time.

Once I began to serve Mass, I fell into the rhythms and patterns of responses and movements. I enjoyed it, the way that I enjoyed the choreography of a game that was played smoothly and with precision. I enjoyed being close to the altar and the mysterious holiness that enveloped it. With some sense of pride and awe mixed together, I felt that I was in a singularly privileged spot. Years later, when I read Rudolf Otto's *The Idea of the Holy*, I understood what was going on in my eleven year old head and heart. Around that altar, I met the *mysterium fascinans et tremendum*, that mystery that draws us close and, at the same time, engenders awe. In the Mass, I knew both the closeness and transcendence of divine mystery.

The Forty Hours' Devotion

Saint Agnes celebrated the Forty Hours' Devotion annually. For some forty hours, the Blessed Sacrament was exposed in a golden monstrance on the altar. The monstrance resembled a sunburst with the pure white host in the center. People would sign up for times to come and keep vigil and pray before the Eucharist. Classes from the school would come in, do a double (two-knee) genuflection because of the exposed sacrament, and then pray for an hour interspersing as they did a little song whose melody never leaves your head once you hear it:

O Sacrament most holy,
O Sacrament divine,
all praise and all thanksgiving
be forever thine!

The sanctuary was brightly lit. On the altar where the monstrance was set, there were many candles. The altar itself was decorated with cascades of flowers and a large gold cloth called an *antependium* that hung, as the word implies, on the front of the altar. I think back now and the whole arrangement seems more akin to a Buddhist temple that you might see on a travel show through Asia than to a Catholic church. Back then, there was no other point of reference, and it was an impressive setting. The Eucharist, the host itself, was the focal point for attention and prayer. We were drawn into a quiet contemplation, a peaceful regard of the presence of Jesus among us. I did not realize then that the Forty Hours' Devotion was introducing me to another dimension of the Eucharist—contemplative centering, focusing, resting, remaining with, as Saint Teresa of Avila once said, "the one we know who loves us."

The service concluding the Forty Hours' required a full phalanx of altar boys. We had little to do. We served a mainly decorative purpose. The closing celebration was spirited and involved a procession around the church and the singing of the Litany of the Saints, a very long list of saints sung in Latin, name by Latin name, generally recognizable but sometimes barely so. After each name, the whole congregation sang *ora pro nobis*—"pray for us." The effect was hypnotic. As an altar boy, I had a front row seat and, one year, got a good, close look at the priest who was belting out—and he was really belting it out—the names in the Litany of the Saints. His face was as red as anything I had ever seen and his enthusiastic invocations were shaking the windows of the place. Later, I came to know that the pastor held a huge party before the service for the priests in attendance at the Forty Hours'. And there was plenty to eat and not a little to drink. But there was nothing scandalous in this. In my own way, I came to associate the Eucharist with an unusual combination of quiet contemplation and enthusiastic exuberance. That was the Forty Hours' experience.

Early Years in the Seminary

I was ready for high school and decided that I wanted to become a priest. In 1958, making that kind of decision at a young age was not unusual. My experience of the Eucharist certainly played an important part in that decision, and the encouragement of the sisters who taught me confirmed it. I enrolled in Quigley Preparatory Seminary, a day school run by the Archdiocese of Chicago for boys who wanted to become priests. We were told at the very beginning that an essential part of the program was participation in daily Mass. I accepted that and began a practice of daily Mass which has remained with me for fifty-three years.

In my high school years, I had an hour and a half commute from my home to the seminary each day. I left the house at 6:30 AM and arrived at the Quigley chapel for Mass at 8 AM. Participation in daily Mass became an essential rhythm of my life. I think now that when I was younger there were some obsessive elements of that practice, and that is not uncommon in the development of an adolescent's spirituality. What grew within me, however, was a sense that the

Mass was an anchor in my life, a point of reference that was steady and reliable.

Because we had some special instruction in liturgy and because we used hand-held missals (not the rocket-launcher kind but the small prayer books that replicated the book that the priest used on the altar), I learned more about the Mass. Probably, the greatest lesson I learned from the routine of daily Mass was about time—a new way of thinking about time and actually living out time. For a teenager, time is a strange jumble of endless hours that go on and on and, in just another moment,

> **Probably, the greatest lesson I learned from the routine of daily Mass was about time—a new way of thinking about time and actually living out time.**

a quick or speeding succession of disjointed experiences. The daily liturgy brought me into another sphere. At the beginning of each day, the Eucharist or Mass offered a direction for the day's unfolding. The liturgical seasons gave me another sense of time. From Advent through Christmas and then Lent and Easter and Ordinary Time—with the particular notes of the seasons of expectation, fulfillment, repentance, and joy—there was real movement, not just endless days, each one like the other. I learned to enter time differently with a sense of flow, coherence, and direction. It was a blessing of the Eucharist that stays with me today.

As I continued in high school and began college seminary, the years coincided with preparations for the Second Vatican Council and for the sessions of the Council itself. Liturgy was the first order of business for the Council, and the document on the renewal of the liturgy was the first document of the Council to be promulgated on December 4, 1963. In those years, I remember reading *Worship,* a journal dedicated to liturgy edited by the monks of Saint John's Abbey in Collegeville, Minnesota. I remember reading articles about liturgy in *Jubilee,* a magazine of Catholic culture and trends that counted Thomas Merton among its regular contributors. I felt excitement in these writings and a sense of promise. The renewal of the liturgy had nothing to do with discarding the past, what we had developed and understood for two thousand years. The point was to deepen our sense of worship, especially of the Eucharist, and to make it more accessible to the whole Church. That experience surrounding the Council and even the many "liturgy wars" of these many years after the Council, taught me that the unchanging gift of the Eucharist comes to us in different—and sometimes adequate and sometimes less adequate—circumstances. I sensed early on that liturgical and eucharistic renewal must always in some way involve retrieval— going back and getting at the heart of the matter which can so easily be lost.

Around the same time in my college years of seminary, I reclaimed another link that had long been forged in the Church in Chicago—the link between the Eucharist and justice, between the eucharistic Body of Christ and care for the Church as the Body of Christ, especially the poor. For several summers during college, I worked with Father Fidel Rodriguez, a Spanish Augustinian. Father Fidel organized a summer school for the children of migrant workers who came to harvest vegetables in the south end of Cook County. They were Mexicans, whole families, on the move from harvest to harvest around the country. And they were very poor. The children of these workers consequently had a fragmented educational experience. The summer school was meant to help them catch up. Wisely, Father Fidel knew that the children needed more than spelling and arithmetic. They also needed religious education. Our program provided remedial work in traditional school subjects and religious education, especially preparation for the Sacraments of Penance and Holy Communion.

When these migrant children celebrated their First Holy Communion—girls in Communion dresses and veils and boys in white shirts and ties—there was great joy, as there always is at First Holy Communion, but perhaps even more so here. This Eucharist meant triumph over adversity. It meant possession of the dignity and esteem that belong to all God's people, especially the poor. It meant that many people in the Church had shared their gifts to make the day happen. It meant that we were in this together. The entire *fiesta* represented the culmination of a commitment of people of faith to stand for justice and dignity for the poor. And all this happened appropriately in the context of the Eucharist. My eyes were opened.

Studies in Rome

I did my final four years of preparation for ordination by studying theology in Rome at the Gregorian University and living at the North American College, a few hundred feet from Saint Peter's Square. Across those four years, in Rome and other places in Europe, I experienced the Eucharist in new, beautiful, and moving circumstances. I studied the Eucharist at the Gregorian University with two Jesuit professors, Father Louis Ligier who represented the French scholarship of the twentieth century in the area of sacramental theology, and the liturgist Father Herman Schmidt, a very big Dutchman, who stood in the great line of German liturgical scholarship. Later, in 1973, when I was doing graduate work and had completed my courses, I audited a course on the Eucharist offered by a visiting professor, Father Joseph Ratzinger. He was deep and clear in probing questions across the centuries concerning the Eucharist, but, above all, he presented himself as a committed believer who drew life from this sacrament.

While the formal academic study of the Eucharist sharpened my appreciation of the sacrament, the actual celebrations of the Eucharist left a deeper imprint on my soul. There were many celebrations, but several stand out.

On the feast of Pentecost in 1969, Pope Paul VI invited all the seminarians studying in Rome to Saint Peter's Basilica for Mass. It was an extraordinary assembly that represented the nations, cultures, and languages of the entire world. Readings, prayers, and music reflected our diversity, and the Eucharist itself was the dramatic and unforgettable point of unity. And all this took place in the church built over the tomb of Peter, a place where he and other saints were buried, a place of pilgrimage across two thousand years.

I left that Mass deeply moved and aware of the Holy Spirit who in the Eucharist links believers all around the world from the rising of the sun to its setting; the Holy Spirit who links believers in the great communion of saints, those on earth and those in heaven. The power of that particular Mass has remained with me, and it has made me aware that every Mass links us together across the world, across time, and between heaven and earth.

Later that same year on December 19th, I was ordained a priest in Saint Peter's and then celebrated my first Mass the next day in a convent chapel just off of Saint Peter's Square. Of course, that Mass is indelibly marked in my memory, and it was a joyous event. In retrospect, however, I was too self-conscious, too concerned about the proper way to celebrate Mass to allow it to have the spiritual impact that other Masses would have in my priesthood, including some that shortly followed it in Rome.

As I finished my studies after ordination and before my return to the United States between January and July of 1970, I celebrated Mass at Carlo Forlanini Hospital in Rome. More precisely, I celebrated Mass in the orthopedic pavilion. The patients in this part of the hospital came from different parts of Italy and were hospitalized for extended periods, ranging from several months to several years. Most of them were in the hospital because of botched medical procedures that resulted in significant damage to their bones and often required either partial or full body casts. No one could clearly predict how much time recovery would take or even if the treatments would work. Additionally, patients had to cope with the absence of their families, who lived at a distance.

Several religious sisters were in charge of nursing in this part of the hospital. Along with the physicians and other staff, they somehow miraculously created and sustained a community of positive hope and compassion. The sisters helped me, newly ordained and the new kid on the block, to navigate the celebration of the Mass and the follow-up visits with patients. I am forever indebted to them and to the patients whom I served in those first months of my priesthood.

I was awkward at the altar and my preaching was positively numbing—I have saved my notes as well as the memory of several patients snoring loudly during my homilies. For all that, I encountered the power of the Eucharist in a new and utterly transformative way. Among suffering people who were uncertain about their futures, I discovered hope across the altar. The patients were very simple people who could not afford private clinics. They were in a public hospital. With little fuss and no ability to articulate their experience theologically, they knew and they lived the Eucharist as the great sacrament of hope, the hope that only God can give to sustain his people. The Masses at Carlo Forlanini left me astonished. And more than forty years later, I am still amazed at the faith of people and the power of the Eucharist.

Returning Home

I returned home to the Archdiocese of Chicago, and for the past four decades have served here and celebrated Mass here. My service began at Our Lady of the Angels Church, the place where a tragic school fire in 1958 had claimed the lives of ninety children and three teaching sisters. I arrived there twelve years later, and of course the scars of that experience remained. The neighborhood, however, was changing demographically. During my time there, the parish was trilingual and multicultural: English, Italian, and Spanish. It was perplexing and, at times, exhausting to hold this community together. The shifting demographics, the introduction at that time of the "new" Mass, and the cultural spillover of the 1960s into the early 1970s made everything challenging. In this maelstrom, the Mass remained a steady factor, even when celebrated poorly or strangely for the sake of "relevance." I learned that the Mass was not only a resource in Life's challenges but that the Mass itself could be challenging, as we struggled to stay centered and connected. It was not easy.

I had other parish experiences, but the largest block of time—twenty-two years—was devoted to teaching in the major seminary of the Archdiocese of Chicago. I found that the seminary was not so different from the parishes. The seminary was deeply affected by the shifts in the culture. The seminary struggled to find its way through liturgical renewal. The seminary needed to re-appropriate the centrality of the Eucharist, a focus that could be fragile and easily lost. Slowly and surely, the seminary and its entire program began to be more and more grounded in a eucharistic center. Again, I learned that the Eucharist is a gift, the supreme gift, given to us by the Lord, and it is also our responsibility. And that responsibility may entail a struggle to respond to the gift.

In the Parish

After thirty-five years of serving as a priest as a seminary professor or associate pastor, I became the pastor of my own parish, Divine Savior in Norridge, Illinois. My nearly four years of being a pastor drew me into the mystery of the Eucharist in new and surprising ways.

I found that celebrating Mass for my people was a joyful and, at times, even an exhilarating experience. I also quickly discovered a whole new set of eucharistic responsibilities that belonged to me, because I was the pastor. When I was a faculty member of the seminary, I celebrated Mass on weekends in parishes. For nearly twenty-two years, I celebrated Mass at Saint Edward's parish on the northwest side of Chicago. I really loved that experience, and I loved the people of that parish. Although I only had contact with the people there on weekends, I felt a great closeness and attachment to the parishioners. Praying together at Mass and celebrating the Mass as a priest are acts of great intimacy. We come together with our vulnerabilities and gifts, our hopes and our struggles. We bring everything—down to the smallest and deepest detail of our lives—to

> We come together with our vulnerabilities and gifts, our hopes and our struggles. We bring everything—down to the smallest and deepest detail of our lives—to the altar and join ourselves to Jesus who offers himself to the Father for our sake.

the altar and join ourselves to Jesus who offers himself to the Father for our sake. That is the intimacy. As close as I was to the people of Saint Edward's, I found that things shifted internally for me when I celebrated Mass for my own people at Divine Savior as their pastor.

As a pastor I felt a special responsibility to help my people draw life from the Eucharist. This may sound overly dramatic or perhaps exaggerated. It was not. As their teacher and spiritual guide, I wanted them to know, to be convinced, and to live the words of Jesus: "I am the living bread that came down from heaven. Whoever eats of this bread will live forever; and the bread that I will give for the life of the world is my flesh" (John 6:51). My first inclination to help parishioners arrive at that knowledge, conviction, and commitment was to teach them, that is, to lecture to them. After all, I was an experienced teacher in the classroom. With the Holy Spirit's inspiration, I resisted the temptation to go theoretical. My people overall were not theoretical, and even those who were, I discerned, would probably not be moved by words about the Eucharist. So instead of theoretical teaching, I decided that I would communicate the meaning, the possibilities, and the practical implications of the Eucharist through my way of celebrating the Mass itself. I tried, as best as I could, to prepare myself for every celebration of Mass in the parish from the most ordinary weekday Mass at 7:30 AM, to the most solemn feasts and everything between. In some measure it worked, but not perfectly. By the time I left the parish, there was still more eucharistic formation to be done, but we had made some progress together.

Parishes of their very nature consist of good-hearted people. Divine Savior was no exception. These assemblies of the good-hearted, however, can also be rife with petty jealousies and divisions. Again, Divine Savior was no exception. This meant that I shared Paul's frustration with the Corinthian community concerning its eucharistic inconsistency, that is, celebrating their unity in Jesus Christ but living their life together in fractured ways. It is not enough, I discovered, for a pastor to preach well and to celebrate the Eucharist well. The pastor must also be concerned about how the Eucharist is lived in the community. With regularity—in parish meetings or personal encounters or bulletin articles—I stood as a reminder for eucharistic integrity and consistency, to live out in our lives what we had celebrated at the altar. There will always be a mismatch between celebration and living. It is our condition as a pilgrim people who are on the way but who have not yet arrived. Still, as their pastor I wanted to help my people to narrow the gap as much as we could with God's help.

One of the most complex and complicated experiences in the parish was the First Holy Communion for our second graders in religious education (we had no school). Preparation of the children signaled a high point for me. I enjoyed being with them in the classroom and reinforcing the lessons that their catechists were imparting to them. They were consistently eager learners and joyful, as they prepared to receive Jesus for the first time in Holy Communion. That was a delightful and uplifting experience. Sadly, the actual celebration of First Holy Communion, at least a couple of times, turned out to be very painful. Families came armed with cameras and determination to chronicle the event. Many of the adults spoke loudly during the Mass and gave evidence that they were very unfamiliar with being in church during the celebration of Mass. I am certain that most of those who came to the First Communion would have identified themselves as Catholics. Yet most of those who came were marginally connected with the Catholic Church and certainly participated rarely in the Mass except for First Communions, marriages, and funerals.

This experience with all its contrasts and contradictions jarred me. It also alerted me to a troubling phenomenon which I fear will only grow. As more Catholics drift from the Church and the practice of their faith but continue to claim Catholic identity much as they might some cultural identity, they will disregard and interrupt significant sacred moments in a way that is utterly offensive for people of faith. They will do so because they are profoundly ignorant of the faith to which they claim allegiance.

A related incident, that caused me to want to laugh and cry at the same time, occurred when a young woman came to the rectory to plan her father's funeral Mass. Practically the first words out her mouth were, "I don't want any of this death stuff at my father's funeral. I want it to be a celebration of his life." I assured her that it would be difficult to avoid facing death in the presence of the casket with her father's remains. I also tried to explain that the funeral Mass was a prayer for her father and an affirmation of our belief and hope in the power of the Risen Lord who conquers death and brings us to eternal life. Perhaps in some small way, that awkward dialogue led the young woman to some deeper understanding, but I was not certain.

The regular Sunday celebrations of the Mass continued to be powerful and sustaining for me. People regularly shared their gratitude and appreciation for our worship. There was nothing elaborate about these Masses. They were celebrated in a very humble church building with simple music. Word and sacrament, however, carried a power to nourish people spiritually and sustain them in hope. Precisely because of the positive celebrations of the Eucharist, I found it distasteful to serve as a "gate-keeper" for the Eucharist in other contexts. I did it, however, because I felt that the holy mysteries would otherwise be treated as commonplace, because the sacred would irretrievably be melded into the profane. Here, for example, are two paragraphs from a bulletin article that explains what I did to watch over the Eucharist and what happened as a result of that:

> If you will recall, a few weeks ago I wrote in a bulletin article about a practice I instituted here at Divine Savior for funerals and weddings. Just before the distribution of Holy Communion, I say, "Now we will have the distribution of Holy Communion. If you are Catholic and if you are prepared, please come forward at this time. If not, I invite you to remain in the pew." In that article, I explained my reasoning for saying this. My rationale includes: (a) a courtesy for non-Catholics who may not be familiar with Catholic rituals; (b) an affirmation that participating in Holy Communion represents participation in the Catholic Church and the acceptance of the integral

faith of the Church; (c) a reminder to Catholics that they must be properly disposed to receive this most holy sacrament worthily and that they never take their participation in Holy Communion lightly or as a matter of routine.

I have discovered in the intervening weeks that people do read the bulletin, that they do hear what I say at funerals and weddings, and that some people—especially Catholics who have drifted from the Church or even joined other churches—are deeply offended and disturbed by my words. In one recent conversation, for example, a young lady quite emphatically told me, "I don't practice the faith, but I do believe in God. And I have a right to receive Holy Communion if I want to." Well, of course, I could affirm belief in God as a positive. There is, however, a big difference between believing God as I might personally conceive God and being a part of the Catholic Church. She saw no difference. I told her that she was scripting her own religion. She disagreed. She had been raised Catholic and felt that she was a good one, even though she rarely practiced her faith in a public way. Without judging her state of soul—that belongs to God not to me—I think it can be safely said that she may be a good person but not a good Catholic who was ready to participate freely in the Eucharist.

I do not think that there is anything more unpleasant than to have these kinds of conversations in which people think that I am judging them, excluding them, and—in a highhanded way—diminishing them. My point and my commitment is to stay with the truth of the Eucharist and to uphold that truth. I tried to do it gently and kindly but also clearly. And at every step of the way, I felt my eucharistic responsibility to call people to deeper understanding and commitment to the Eucharist.

I want to conclude the sharing of my experience of the Eucharist as the pastor of a parish with a note about care for the dying. Although I have never verified it, someone once told me that Norridge, Illinois, where Divine Savior Church is located, has the densest population of senior citizens in northern Illinois. I can confidently say that we had a number of deaths that was quite disproportionate to the size of the parish. An important part of my ministry, therefore, was initiating people into the Christian *ars moriendi*, literally, the art of dying or, better translated, preparing to die well. The Eucharist played an important role in teaching people the *ars moriendi*. Jesus himself said, "Those who eat my flesh and drink my blood have eternal life, and I will raise them up on the last day; . . . This is the bread that came down from heaven, not like that which your ancestors ate, and they died. But the one who eats this bread will live forever" (John 6: 54, 58). I also took my cue from the chant authored by Saint Thomas Aquinas: *O sacrum convivium, in quo Christus sumitur; recolitur memoria passionis eius: mens impletur gratia: et futurae gloriae nobis pignus datur.* " O sacred banquet, wherein Christ is received; the memory of his passion is renewed, the mind is filled with grace, and the pledge of future glory is given unto us."

From the time of the Fathers in the Eastern Church, the Eucharist has been called *to pharmakon tes athanasias*, "the medicine of immortality." Although I knew theoretically that the Eucharist was the food of eternal life, the experience of helping my parishioners prepare for death brought me to a new depth of appreciation of the Eucharist as the bread of Resurrection, as the pledge of future glory, and as the medicine of immortality. In preaching and teaching, during hospital visits, and in visits to homebound people, I carried this message, which had fresh and powerful meaning for me.

Because of hospice care, more and more people are spending their final days at home and dying there. Some of the most moving experiences of my entire priestly ministry happened in the care of dying parishioners in their homes surrounded by their loved ones. On many occasions I was privileged to give the dying Viaticum, their last Holy Communion. The word *Viaticum* means "food for the journey." This last Eucharist sustains dying persons in their passage from this life through death to eternal life. Early on in my tenure as pastor, Rosaria Principato showed me the power of Viaticum.

Rosaria had been a part of a prayer group. She was an immigrant who knew the hardships of leaving one's native land and forging a new life in strange and unfamiliar circumstances. She was also a woman of deep faith who never kept that gift as her private possession. She kept her eyes open for those who had strayed from the ways of faith. And she did what she could to bring them back to life in Jesus Christ. When she was diagnosed with ovarian cancer, she was in great pain. In an intentional and deliberate way, she joined her sufferings with those of Jesus, and she offered them for those in need, including me, her pastor. This was a truly holy woman and a person of blessing for all those whom she encountered. In the very last stages of her life, I brought her Viaticum, her last Holy Communion, her food for her journey home. She was surrounded by her husband and devoted family and friends. She was blessed, and we were blessed through her.

As I walked away from Rosaria's home, I recognized how deeply I was touched by her and her faith. I felt a deep sense of privilege in bringing her the last Holy Communion of her life on earth. I saw in a new way how our lives are framed by the Eucharist, how we begin with our First Holy Communion and finish with our last Holy Communion. And in between there are other Holy Communions that continue and sustain the relationship that we have with Jesus. There are other Holy Communions that bring us closer and closer to him who is our hope and to others in him who is our love. How amazing it is, this stretch of union and communion across a lifetime.

As I write these words about Rosaria Principato and her death, I am very conscious of how strange her life and death must seem to many of our contemporaries and how strange my observations must sound. We live either in a mostly secular and skeptical world with its modern and post-modern pretensions, or in a religious/funda-mentalist world that rewrites reality to conform not with some spiri-tual text, but with someone's notion of that text's meaning. What I experienced with Rosaria and others in the parish did not fit with how today's intellectual elites would frame her world. They would say that she lived in an enchanted world of mystification, but she did not. She lived not in an enchanted world but in a world suffused by a loving direction "despite it all." Her experience did not fit the fer-vent worlds of televangelists and others who seem to promise a resolution of all pain and suffering here and now. Rosaria suffered terribly and did not deny it. Overall, the difference that makes her experience (and mine to the extent I shared in hers) rare in the world is the difference of loving relationship. Further, it is relationship with the human and divine in Jesus, who is really encountered in word and sacrament. Everything in Rosaria's experience that coalesced in this relationship, especially in her last days, was summed up in the Eucharist as presence, struggle, connection, love, promise, and hope.

Clearly, this parish part of my eucharistic autobiography stretches the genre of autobiography beyond a single subjectivity, my own, to include a story and a journey shared with others, in communion. While my own eucharistic story began with the dawn of my self-awareness and the beginning of my personal memory, it has moved ineluctably beyond me, inevitably connecting me beyond myself, obviously with the One who is the Eucharist and then in him with others who share the one bread.

Reflections on My Eucharistic Autobiography

I have since moved out of the parish. Now I work for departments and agencies of the Archdiocese of Chicago, and I am a priest in residence at Chicago's Holy Name Cathedral, where I celebrate Mass. My eucharistic autobiography tells me that in this next phase of my ministry and life, my understanding and appreciation of the Eucharist will continue to unfold, and I hope this will be true for my commitment to this great sacrament. My experiences and encounters with the Eucharist stretched across nearly sixty-five years have clearly shown me that I stand before an inexhaustible mystery. In anticipating future developments unfolding, I want to stay alert and ready to receive them when and as they happen.

I also look on this eucharistic autobiography and recognize that it is fundamentally the story of a relationship. This is not the story of my relationship with an object, as if the Eucharist were simply some thing. In fact, my relationship has been deeply and thoroughly personal, because the Eucharist is the personal presence of Jesus. Inevitably, then, my encounters with the Eucharist have always been personal encounters with the Lord in the context of a living relation-ship. With time, the relationship has deepened in ways that have affected every sphere of my life—intellect, emotions, and practical decisions. This fact indicates that it is a very significant relationship that is comprehensive in nature. Other relationships of this kind, for example, two people deeply in love with each other, or a parent/child relationship, cannot be explained or justified with ideas and constructs from a place outside of the relationship. Such relation-ships can be described and analyzed only in limited ways. In their density and complexity, these relationships can only be self-validating. That is exactly how I see my relationship to the Eucharist across the years. Even in describing the way that the relationship has devel-oped I would make no claim that I am explaining it or giving its rationale. The experience, I have come to realize, will forever out-pace my ability even to express it, much less explain it.

Now, in some secular and post-modern quarters, these state-ments may cause dismissive laughter or accusations of mystification or a deficit of clear thinking. There is, I would maintain, a deficit in secularity and post-modernity. And it amounts to an inability to appreciate fully sustained love which is a mystery best expressed through art, poetry, and music. And the mystery of the Eucharist is the mystery of fully sustained love that has been, in fact, best expressed in song and art and verses of Psalms that are themselves poetic pieces.

Over time, my relationship with the Eucharist has changed me. This does not mean that I can identify a steady line of improvement. Certainly there are ways that the Eucharist has made me a "better me." The Eucharist has opened my heart to a greater compassion and a willingness to forgive and a commitment to be an instrument of reconciliation. In other ways, however, the change effected by the Eucharist has made me more aware of the gap between the truly free self-giving Jesus in the Eucharist, and my own narrow world of self-concern; between the steady and faithful real presence of the Lord in the Eucharist, and my own distracted and inconstant pres-ence to him; and between his universal availability in the Eucharist to feed all who come to him, and my own restricted generosity. Even with an awareness of these gaps, I am changed. I recognize a path of future transformation.

This eucharistic autobiography leaves me deeply grateful. The trajectory of grace across my life is clear. In the Eucharist I have been blessed in so many ways. Even so, this autobiography also leaves me a little fearful. This sacrament is, after all, a proclamation of the Death of the Lord until he comes again in glory. At the heart of the sacrament is Jesus' self-sacrificing love unto death. And embedded in that self-sacrificing love are suffering, surrender of control, and self-entrustment to God in a path of abandonment. I know that this is all part of a eucharistic logic of life, some of which I have already experienced but most of which lies ahead on an unclear path. The unknown naturally causes some anxiety. The eucharistic presence of the One who suffered and died and then rose from the dead gives me courage. The unknown future yields to hope in the One whom I have come to know and who knows me.

Conclusion

At the end of this eucharistic autobiography and our reflections upon it, we do well to return to the opening questions: How can the Eucharist help us face and resolve problems that we face today? Is the Eucharist really *that* important? What can the Eucharist mean for people today? Although we will revisit these questions as we draw from the Word of God in the Bible and the teachings of the Church, I can begin to respond to them in light of my personal experience of the Eucharist.

How can the Eucharist help us resolve problems and difficulties that we face? People rightly expect their faith and their religion to be a source of solace and comfort as they navigate the difficult waters of life. While solace and comfort are important dimensions of our experience of faith, they do not encompass the entire experience of faith which can, in critical moments, be discomforting and challenging, even as it affords hope. This has been my experience.

The Eucharist has been a strong source of solace for me. That solace has resided in the abiding sacramental presence of the Lord, in the reliable relationship signified in this sacrament and enacted in the self-sacrificing love of Jesus, and in the hope that it sparks in us "the pledge of future glory."

I can also say that the Eucharist has shaken me and challenged me, precisely as I faced problems and difficulties. The Eucharist has been for me an essential source of sustenance or, in the words of the ancient hymn, *cibus viatorum*, "the food of travelers," those who make their pilgrim way. In the face of difficulty, the challenge posed by the Eucharist is the challenge to keep going, to persevere, to not give up, and, finally, to embrace the pilgrim condition of my life on earth. With this sustenance, I do not have an excuse to halt the journey.

The Eucharist is empowerment, and as empowerment it has challenged me. In his farewell discourse, Jesus promised the Spirit whom he would send from the Father. The Spirit then would enable Jesus to live within the hearts of believers and enable them to act in this world in his name, continuing his mission and in mysterious ways surpassing the works of his earthly ministry. *"Very truly, I tell you, the one who believes in me will also do the works that I do and, in fact, will do greater works than these, because I am going to the Father"* (John 14:12). That internalization of the presence of Jesus by the power of the Holy Spirit and the empowerment to act in his name coalesces in the Eucharist taken within us in Holy Communion. And here is the challenge. It is a challenge to act, to take hold of this world, and to continue the mission of Jesus. With this empowerment, I do not have an excuse to remain inactive and passive.

The Eucharist is Jesus' great act of eternal intercession in the heavenly sanctuary on our behalf. That Jesus is "for us," "for me" clearly emerges in my experience of Eucharist. This is affirmed in the letter to the Hebrews: *" . . . he is able for all time to save those who approach God through him, since he always lives to make intercession for them"* (Hebrews 7:25). With this intercession present in the Eucharist, I am challenged to believe both that nothing is unsalvageable and that I am called to submit all things to the power of his intercession. With this intercession, I do not have an excuse to surrender to whatever seems to be overwhelming or even ultimately destructive.

Our opening question about the Eucharist asked, *How does the Eucharist help us resolve problems and difficulties that we face?* In my experience, the answer to that question is complex. A partial response must, of course, identify the Eucharist as a fundamental source of solace and comfort. At the same time, the Eucharist challenges us in the face of problems and difficulties, because the Eucharist gives us sustenance to persevere, because the Eucharist empowers us to take action, and because the Eucharist gives us access to the saving intercession of Jesus. Clearly, the Eucharist is not magic power that we can manipulate for our own ends. Everything about the Eucharist draws us into the presence and relationship that we have with Jesus Christ. Everything is personal.

Our second opening question was: Is *the Eucharist really* that *important?* This was a question of relevance, importance, and value. As I gather the elements of my eucharistic autobiography, I can offer an unequivocal *yes* to that question. In fact, from my experience of the Eucharist, I cannot even understand the question itself. How can it be posed? Of course, the Eucharist is *that* important. How could it be otherwise? And yet people, more precisely, more than seventy-five percent of Catholics in the United States raise the question by not participating regularly in the Mass. They are, in effect, saying that it is not that important. How could they come to that conclusion? There may be a key in my own autobiographical musings.

The central and critical importance of the Eucharist for me emerged, as I think my autobiography identifies it, over time with contact and growing communion. This ought not surprise us. All significant and truly intimate relationships—the ones that assume a central position in our lives—only become that because there has been a shared history, because there has been steady connection, because there has been a time of testing and re-affirmation, because an ease of contact or familiarity has grown, and finally, because there has been a communion of life. So, the critical importance of the Eucharist happened for me, because the Eucharist *became* important at important junctures of my life and in the ordinary rhythms of daily life. I understand how those who have not had this blessed experience would neither know the Eucharist nor find it *that* important. There is a circularity here in the logic of this relationship: it is central because it becomes central; it remains peripheral because it remains peripheral. The spiritual or formational challenge is to break into this circle of relationship and begin to practice familiarity.

Our third initial question was: *What can the Eucharist mean for people today?* From my autobiographical reflections, I can begin to answer this question. For me but beyond me and for my contemporaries, the Eucharist can be connection, hope, and life—as it has been for me. This triad, in my estimation, catches the essential search and question of people today, something that eludes them and that they desperately want. Connections, for example, seem easy with electronic communications, but they are not. People remain isolated on the other side of a computer screen or cell phone. Hope is what politicians talk about but rarely provide. In fact, there are no real purveyors of hope at work in the world. At best, we have an array of escapes or coping devices, which are more or less effective and some of which, like drugs and addictive habits, are ultimately destructive. What about life itself? We dwell in a world beset with micro and macro death-dealing forces. Many people have settled for trying to prolong life medically and, when that does not work, to deny death.

As I consider my own story that is inevitably linked with a moment in history and culture that I share with many other people, I know my longings and theirs as well. That is why I can say with confidence that there are very deep yearnings at work to find connection, hope, and life in a world which affords little if any of these elements. In contrast, I stand before my experience of the Eucharist. Here I find an abundance of connection, hope, and life. In fact, I find such abundance that my small soul cannot absorb it all. There is no question but that the Eucharist, if known and experienced, can mean everything to people today.

Questions for Reflection and Sharing

3.   *Sitting down and doing a complete eucharistic autobiography may seem to be a very challenging task, perhaps simply too difficult to do. The best way to approach your own eucharistic autobiography is to begin it in a limited way. Think back on your life and your experience of the Eucharist. Can you identify two or three moments when your sharing in the Eucharist meant something very special to you? Sharing your response to this question with others will probably open up additional important experiences. Gradually, you will fill out your own eucharistic autobiography.*

4.   *How would you like to move forward in your appreciation of the Eucharist, as you continue your life's journey?*

Part Two

Chapter 3

The Question of the Eucharist in Chapter Six of John's Account of the Gospel

As I noted in the introduction, if we want to understand the meaning and importance of the Eucharist, it is not enough to measure it by our own experience. We do well to pursue another question: *What did Jesus want to give us when he gave us the Eucharist?* It is a matter of coming to know the mind and heart of Jesus. There are many places in the Gospel where Jesus speaks about the Eucharist either directly or through images and actions. One particularly rich resource for understanding the eucharistic intentions of Jesus is chapter six of John's account of the Gospel.

> After this Jesus went to the other side of the Sea of Galilee, also called the Sea of Tiberias. A large crowd kept following him, because they saw the signs that he was doing for the sick. Jesus went up the mountain and sat down there with his disciples. Now the Passover, the festival of the Jews, was near. When he looked up and saw a large crowd coming towards him, Jesus said to Philip, **"Where are we to buy bread for these people to eat?"** He said this to test them, for he himself knew what he was going to do. (John 6:1–6)

> Philip answered him, "Six months' wages would not buy enough bread for each of them to get a little." One of his disciples, Andrew,

Simon Peter's brother, said to him, "There is a boy here who has five barley loaves and two fish. **But what are they among so many people?** (John 6:7–9)

Jesus said, "Make the people sit down." Now there was a great deal of grass in the place; so they sat down, about five thousand in all. Then Jesus took the loaves, and when he had given thanks, he distributed them to those who were seated; so also the fish, as much as they wanted. When they were satisfied, he told his disciples, "Gather up the fragments left over, so that nothing may be lost." So they gathered them up, and from the fragments of the five barley loaves, left by those who had eaten, they filled twelve baskets. When the people saw the sign that he had done, they began to say, "This is indeed the prophet who is to come into the world."

When Jesus realized that they were about to come and take him by force to make him king, he withdrew again to the mountain by himself. (John 6:10–15)

When evening came, his disciples went down to the lake, got into a boat, and started across the lake to Capernaum. It was now dark, and Jesus had not yet come to them. The lake became rough because a strong wind was blowing. When they had rowed about three or four miles, they saw Jesus walking on the lake and coming near the boat, and they were terrified. But he said to them, "It is I; do not be afraid." Then they wanted to take him into the boat, and immediately the boat reached the land towards which they were going.

The next day the crowd that had stayed on the other side of the lake saw that there had been only one boat there. They also saw that Jesus had not got into the boat with his disciples, but that his disciples had gone away alone. Then some boats from Tiberias came near the place where they had eaten the bread after the Lord had given thanks. So when the crowd saw that neither Jesus nor his disciples were there, they themselves got into the boats and went to Capernaum looking for Jesus.

When they found him on the other side of the lake, they said to him, "**Rabbi, when did you come here?**" Jesus answered them, "Very truly I tell you, you are looking for me, not because you saw signs, but because you ate your fill of the loaves. Do not work for the food that perishes, but for the food that endures for eternal life, which the Son of Man will give you. For it is on him that God the Father has set his seal." (John 6: 16–27)

Then they said to him, "**What must we do to perform the works of God**?" Jesus answered them, "This is the work of God, that you believe in him whom he has sent." (John 6:28–29)

So they said to him, "**What sign are you going to give us then, so that we may see it and believe in you? What work are you performing?** Our ancestors ate the manna in the wilderness, as it is written, 'He gave them bread from heaven to eat.'" Then Jesus said to them, "Very truly, I tell you, it was not Moses who gave you the bread from heaven, but it is my Father who gives you the true bread from heaven. For the bread of God is that which comes down from heaven and gives life to the world." (John 6:30–33)

They said to him, "Sir, give us this bread always." Jesus said to them, "I am the bread of life. Whoever comes to me will never be hungry, and whoever believes in me will never be thirsty. But I said to you that you have seen me and yet do not believe. Everything that the Father gives me will come to me, and anyone who comes to me I will never drive away; for I have come down from heaven, not to do my own will but the will of him who sent me. And this is the will of him who sent me, that I should lose nothing of all that he has given me, but raise it up on the last day. This is indeed the will of my Father, that all who see the Son and believe in him may have eternal life; and I will raise them up on the last day." (John 6:34–40)

Then the Jews began to complain about him because he said, "I am the bread that came down from heaven." They were saying, "**Is not this Jesus, the son of Joseph, whose father and mother we know? How can he now say, "I have come down from heaven"?** Jesus answered them, "Do not complain among yourselves. No one can come to me unless drawn by the Father who sent me; and I will raise that person up on the last day. It is written in the prophets, "And they shall all be taught by God." Everyone who has heard and learned from the father comes to me. Not that anyone has seen the Father except the one who is from God; he has seen the Father. Very truly, I tell you, whoever believes has eternal life. (John 6:41–47)

"I am the bread of life. Your ancestors ate the manna in the wilderness, and they died. This is the bread that comes down from heaven, so that one may eat of it and not die. I am the living bread that came down from heaven. Whoever eats of this bread will live for ever;

and the bread that I will give for the life of the world is my flesh." The Jews then disputed among themselves, saying, **"How can this man give us his flesh to eat?"** So Jesus said to them, "Very truly, I tell you, unless you eat the flesh of the Son of Man and drink his blood, you have no life in you. (John 6:48–53)

"Those who eat my flesh and drink my blood have eternal life, and I will raise them up on the last day; for my flesh is true food and my blood is true drink. Those who eat my flesh and drink my blood abide in me, and I in them. Just as the living Father sent me, and I live because of the Father, so whoever eats me will live because of me. This is the bread that came down from heaven, not like that which your ancestors ate, and they died. But the one who eats this bread will live for ever." He said these things while he was teaching in the synagogue at Capernaum. (John 6:54–59)

When many of his disciples heard it, they said, **"This teaching is difficult; who can accept it?"** But Jesus, being aware that his disciples were complaining about it, said to them, **"Does this offend you? Then what if you were to see the Son of Man ascending to where he was before?"** It is the spirit that gives life; the flesh is useless. The words that I have spoken to you are spirit and life. But among you there are some who do not believe." For Jesus knew from the first who were the ones that did not believe, and who was the one that would betray him. And he said, "For this reason I have told you that no one can come to me unless it is granted by the Father." (John 6:60–65)

And he said, "For this reason I have told you that no one can come to me unless it is granted by the Father." Because of this many of his disciples turned back and no longer went about with him. So Jesus asked the twelve, "Do you also wish to go away?" Simon Peter answered him, "Lord, to whom can we go? You have the words of eternal life. We have come to believe and know that you are the Holy One of God." Jesus answered them, "Did I not choose you, the twelve? Yet one of you is a devil." He was speaking of Judas son of Simon Iscariot, for he, though one of the twelve, was going to betray him. (John 6:60–65)

At the heart of the sixth chapter of John's account of the Gospel, is Jesus' speaking of himself as the Bread of Life. In Christian tradition and especially in the liturgical life of the Church, this chapter has served as a fundamental resource for understanding the Eucharist. Chapter six is an especially long chapter that contains seventy-one verses. It can be divided in various ways, but three major sections seem clear: the feeding of the five thousand (verses 1–15), Jesus walking on the water (verses 16–21), and Jesus identifying himself as the Bread of Life (verses 21–71).

Chapter six of John's account of the Gospel contains many themes woven together in a single text. Biblical scholars attempt to explain its complicated history of composition and offer various interpretations of particular parts of the text.[1] Our consideration of the text will certainly take into account the results of scholarly research, but we will focus more intently on how the text enlightens our understanding of the Eucharist today. We began with contemporary questions about the Eucharist and then explored the question of the personal meaning of the Eucharist through eucharistic autobiography. And now surprisingly, this fundamental text for understanding the Eucharist in the sixth chapter of John abounds with questions, some fourteen of them. Each question in the text can advance our understanding and appreciation of the Eucharist. I propose to examine each question in the text. All of them together express perennial and constant concerns in the life of the Church and in the faith experience of individual believers. Be aware, however, that the examination of each question in the text will not allow us to examine every detail of the chapter. Still, our reflections, mainly limited to the questions in the chapter, can advance our understanding of the great sacrament of the Eucharist as well help us to identify a context for today's questions.

These questions not only lead us to know more about the Eucharist but, more importantly, they draw us into deeper faith in him who is present in the Eucharist.

Consider the general direction of the questions in chapter six of John's account of the Gospel. They reflect universal elements of human searching for religious meaning and spiritual sustenance.

These same questions, in their context, serve to unfold Jesus' self-revelation. These questions not only lead us to know more about the Eucharist but, more importantly, they draw us into deeper faith in him who is present in the Eucharist. Finally, as we move through the text of chapter six with a focus on its questions, we should also bring the questions and experiences that emerge from our personal eucharistic autobiography. We should also bring the larger opening questions of our time to our reflections on this text. In this way, we can let the biblical text about the Eucharist be in dialogue with our personal experience of the Eucharist and with the questions and challenges concerning the Eucharist faced by our contemporaries.

Chapter Six of John's Account of the Gospel: Text and Commentary on Its Questions

> After this Jesus went to the other side of the Sea of Galilee, also called the Sea of Tiberias. A large crowd kept following him, because they saw the signs that he was doing for the sick. Jesus went up the mountain and sat down there with his disciples. Now the Passover, the festival of the Jews, was near. When he looked up and saw a large crowd coming towards him, Jesus said to Philip, "**Where are we to buy bread for these people to eat?**" He said this to test them, for he himself knew what he was going to do. (John 6:1–6)

When Jesus asks the question, *"Where are we to buy bread for these people to eat?"* he anticipates a concern and a question of the disciples. In other accounts of the Gospel, the disciples themselves directly present their concern and their question to Jesus.[2] John's text seems to confirm that the question really belongs more to the disciples than to Jesus, when it states, *"He said this to test them. . . ."* It is an important question for this community of disciples. In effect, it raises significant issues: How do we obtain sufficient resources? How do we assume our responsibility? How can we meet our needs and those of others?

The question is simple—*where are we to buy bread for these people to eat?*—and yet it touches on deep levels of what we might call a eucharistic consciousness. The question implies an awareness of need. Although physical hunger is the presenting image, the need is not restricted to bodies in need of nourishment. Our needs are manifold and urgent. We hunger to have them fulfilled. Of course, we need food for basic physical sustenance. We also need human connection, affection, and support to sustain us emotionally and socially. Ultimately, we need the connection with God, for whom we long in our heart's restless pursuit of knowledge and absolute love. And that divine connection is the sustaining connection that under-girds every other dimension of our lives. The need for bread, the need for sustenance, voiced in the question represents a first dimension of eucharistic awareness—a hunger that reaches into the very depths of our lives.

A second element in this question reveals another fundamental aspect of eucharistic consciousness. Jesus asks, *where are we to buy bread . . . ?* The question implies that *we* can meet the need or fulfill the hunger in its many dimensions. We have it within us to do what needs to be done. This raises a further question: is it in our nature to be able to take care of the needs and hungers that we experience? In fact, as we stand honestly before the great and deep needs and hungers of our lives, we know that we do not have the resources to satisfy our hungers or to fill our needs. It will not be our work, and the Eucharist tells us that it is the action of grace, God's gift.

The question is about *buying bread*. The act of buying is an act of exchange. I give money to acquire something. In fact, if the exchange is fair, it must be the exchange of equal value. What I give to obtain something should have the same value as what I obtain. I buy a cup of coffee for $1.50. The money and the coffee should be worth about the same thing. On the other hand, to *buy bread*, that is, to obtain what satisfies the deepest hungers and needs of human beings, is impossible for us. We have nothing to offer in exchange or even of approximate value to obtain that bread, which is full truth and absolute love, the divine presence and connection. If we obtain that bread, it will come to us freely, as a gift. In fact, later in chapter six, the image of manna coming down from heaven appropriately

reflects the gratuitous nature this holy bread. This is nothing that
we can work for, nothing that we can purchase, nothing for which
we can make an exchange. As we probe the question, we must conclude that all is grace, that this bread comes into our lives as an
absolutely free gift.

Philip answered him, "Six months' wages would not buy enough
bread for each of them to get a little." One of his disciples, Andrew,
Simon Peter's brother, said to him, "There is a boy here who has five
barley loaves and two fish. **But what are they among so many
people?**" (John 6:7–9)

Andrew identifies some meager resources to feed the people, but
he immediately deems them insufficient, as he raises the question,
But what are they among so many people? Indeed, the five barley
loaves and the two dried fish are insufficient quantitatively for the
crowd. And qualitatively, they represent very little. Barley bread
and dried fish are food for poor people.

As the story unfolds, Jesus takes these meager resources and
makes them not only sufficient but so abundant that leftovers fill
twelve baskets. The Gospel says that the crowd had *"as much as they
wanted"* and *"they were satisfied"* (verses 11–12). In the action of
Jesus that transforms what is little and insignificant into something
abundant and fully satisfying, we can anticipate a pattern of sacramental signs that touch our lives today. The signs of the sacraments
are little, seemingly insignificant and common, things that belong
to all people including the poor—water, oil, bread, and wine. Indeed,
we can say that there is a poverty that belongs to these sacramental
elements. The signs belong to us and to our world. There is nothing
dramatic or grandiose about them. In fact, quite the opposite—they
could easily be overlooked or even dismissed. The meagerness and
poverty of the signs suggest a link with the pattern of the Incarnation—
the Word becoming flesh and dwelling among us. Paul writes, *"For
you know the generous act of our Lord Jesus Christ, that though he*

was rich, yet for your sakes he became poor, so that by his poverty you might become rich" (2 Corinthians 8:9). In and through the poverty of the Word made flesh, we discover ourselves enriched beyond all imagining. And now in a similar way, these poor signs convey divine power. People are amazed at the abundance that they encounter. They are amazed to find the full satisfaction of their longings and hungers.

We can return to Andrew's question—*But what are they among so many?* By God's power, we know, they are enough, more than enough, abundant, and completely satisfying. And we can carry this thought forward to our experience of the Eucharist. What is this little bit of bread and this small sip of common wine? How can it be enough for so many? How can it be sufficient with the massive needs of wounded and fragile humanity? We believe and come to know that by God's power this little bread and wine becomes the self-giving and self-sacrificing presence of the Holy One of God. Here there is a sufficiency that is never exhausted by human need. Here is abundance beyond our imagining.

The story of the feeding of the five thousand continues.

> Jesus said, "Make the people sit down." Now there was a great deal of grass in the place; so they sat down, about five thousand in all. Then Jesus took the loaves, and when he had given thanks, he distributed them to those who were seated; so also the fish, as much as they wanted. When they were satisfied, he told his disciples, "Gather up the fragments left over, so that nothing may be lost." So they gathered them up, and from the fragments of the five barley loaves, left by those who had eaten, they filled twelve baskets. When the people saw the sign that he had done, they began to say, "This is indeed the prophet who is to come into the world."
>
> When Jesus realized that they were about to come and take him by force to make him king, he withdrew again to the mountain by himself. (John 6:10–15)

Before more questions are asked, before Jesus shares more of his life-giving word, and before he summons his followers to faith in him, they must pass over and through the water. Does this evoke Israel's passage in the Exodus through the sea? Is there something of the waters of Baptism here? Can the rough seas mean the frightening turbulence that we all meet in life? Perhaps it is all of this. Certainly, it is a passage to the other shore where new questions are raised, new challenges are encountered, and new promises and new hope are given.

> When evening came, his disciples went down to the lake, got into a boat, and started across the lake to Capernaum. It was now dark, and Jesus had not yet come to them. The lake became rough because a strong wind was blowing. When they had rowed about three or four miles, they saw Jesus walking on the lake and coming near the boat, and they were terrified. But he said to them, "It is I; do not be afraid." Then they wanted to take him into the boat, and immediately the boat reached the land towards which they were going.
>
> The next day the crowd that had stayed on the other side of the lake saw that there had been only one boat there. They also saw that Jesus had not got into the boat with his disciples, but that his disciples had gone away alone. Then some boats from Tiberias came near the place where they had eaten the bread after the Lord had given thanks. So when the crowd saw that neither Jesus nor his disciples were there, they themselves got into the boats and went to Capernaum looking for Jesus. When they found him on the other side of the lake, they said to him, "**Rabbi, when did you come here?**" Jesus answered them, "Very truly I tell you, you are looking for me, not because you saw signs, but because you ate your fill of the loaves. Do not work for the food that perishes, but for the food that endures for eternal life, which the Son of Man will give you. For it is on him that God the Father has set his seal." (John 6: 16–27)

The question—*Rabbi, when did you come here?*—seems straightforward enough. It also contains an element of surprise. Recall that Jesus fled the crowd, because they wanted to make him king.

Additionally, there is the passage across the water. So, the question needs to be filled out in its context: *Rabbi, when did you come here? Don't you know that we have been looking for you?* The importance of "looking for Jesus" is highlighted in verse 24: *". . . they . . . got into the boats and went to Capernaum looking for Jesus."* They have been seeking him, and now, almost caught by surprise, they have found him. Then the question: *Rabbi, when did you come here?*

Jesus immediately addresses their searching, identifies the kind of searching that it is, redirects it to a more genuine and more authentic path, and offers a word of promise. *Very truly, I tell you, you are looking for me, not because you saw signs, but because you ate your fill of the loaves. Do not work for the food that perishes, but for the food that endures for eternal life, which the Son of Man will give you.* Elsewhere in the Gospel according to John, people look for Jesus or search for him but their searching is either ambiguous or very much misdirected. Early in his ministry, for example, after John the Baptist identifies Jesus as the Lamb of God, two of John's disciples follow Jesus. He turns around, sees them following him, and asks, *"What are you looking for?"* (John 1:38). Whether out of confusion or embarrassment, the two disciples answer with a question of their own: *"Where are you staying?" He said to them, "Come and see"* (John 1:38b–39a). Looking for Jesus also plays a part in a hostile encounter that Jesus has with the Pharisees: *Again, he said them, "I am going away, and you will search for me, but you will die in your sin. Where I am going, you cannot come."* Shortly, he explains that their search will go nowhere and that they will die in their sins *". . . unless you believe that I am he"* (John 8:21, 24).

When did you come here? We have been looking for you. Jesus correctly understands their search. It is not a search for him but for what he gave them, a physically satisfying meal. Their search, he tells them, is for an object, not a person, namely, himself. He redirects them or, more precisely, he redirects their searching. With the Pharisees and their search for him, it is a different matter. They will look for him, Jesus says, but without success, because a true searching means believing in Jesus.

These questions associated with looking for Jesus have great relevance for our eucharistic search. *When did you come here? We have been looking for you.* This can be our question and our declaration. And yet our search or eucharistic quest is not automatically or necessarily well-directed. Our search cannot be for an object of some sort, even a very holy object that we venerate with great respect and deference. At its core, it must be a search for the person of Jesus. If we search for the object and not the person, we make the same mistake the crowd made. Furthermore, it cannot be a search for this person apart from faith and loving attachment, or else we fall into the trap of the Pharisees.

Perhaps we can understand this authentic looking for Jesus in the Eucharist from another perspective, that of the very nature of sacraments. Sacraments are efficacious signs, that is, they effect what they signify. Our own limited human perceptions, however, can render that sacramental reality ambiguous. We can confuse the sign for the signified and so fall short of the full meaning of the sacrament. We grasp the sign but do not fully embrace the personal reality, the presence of Jesus in his self-sacrificing love. Alternately, we are so taken up with the objective reality of the presence of the Lord, that we are unmindful that this is a sacrament of faith that summons us to an ever-deeper faith in him who is present.

Rabbi, when did you come here? We have been looking for you. We hear the question and we understand the searching. In our own eucharistic journey, we recognize that we are doubly summoned to purification and to a deeper, faithful appropriation of the mystery of the sacrament. Our purification entails letting go of the merely objective reality to embrace more fully the personal reality of Jesus present. The deepening appropriation of the mystery means a more and more surrendering reliance on Jesus who leads us into his life through the Eucharist.

Then they said to him, "**What must we do to perform the works of God?**" Jesus answered them, "This is the work of God, that you believe in him whom he has sent." (John 6:28–29)

The crowd that has been looking for Jesus and has finally caught up with him consists—I think we can safely say—of sincere people, sincere searchers, even if, as Jesus indicates, their searching needs to be purified and redirected. Their spiritual searching leads them to ask another question—*what must we do to perform the works of God?* That question comes from their religious sincerity. It also comes from a very human propensity to figure out how *we* can achieve what we want to see happen. We take ourselves seriously, and we claim responsibility for results, even very spiritual results like performing the works of God.

Again, Jesus takes their question and, in his response, turns their query around in an entirely different direction. He says, "*This is the work of God, that you believe in him whom he has sent.*" The starting point, he says in effect, is not what you do but what God has already done in sending Jesus. That is the great work of God. And those who wish to be a part of this work of God can do so by believing what God has done and believing in the One whom he has sent. Furthermore, that *believing in him* means first accepting the truth of the mission of the Son of God, that indeed God has sent him. *Believing in him* also means relying on him and trusting in him, the one whom God has sent. This second sense of believing leads to a new and transformed way of living, because now life is lived in conjunction and in communion with the one whom God has sent.

We might ask ourselves, "How does this question about 'doing the works of God' have an impact on our own sense of the Eucharist today?" The question of the crowd is our question as well. *What must we do to perform the works of God?* This question belongs to those who want to live righteous and good lives, to people who want to accomplish the will of God in their lives. Even if they are aware of their own fragility and even inconstancy in living out "the works of God," their hearts—and our hearts as well—are set on that goal.

The response of Jesus to this critical question of our lives comes both in his words and in the Eucharist itself. When he says, "*This is the work of God, that you believe in him whom he has sent,*" he shifts our focus in two ways. We come to understand that it is not a matter of many *works* but of a single and singular *work*. We also come to understand that it is not a matter of *our works for God* but rather the prior *work of God for us* in sending the Son among us. Our response to God's work and our participation in it begins with faith, our acceptance of the work of God.

The verbal response of Jesus to the crowd—*This is the work of God, that you believe in him whom he has sent*—echoes today in our experience of the Eucharist. Our primary experience of the Eucharist, whether in the action of the liturgy or in the contemplative prayer of adoration, is not that the Eucharist is one of our works. On the contrary, the Eucharist is the work of God given to us. And our language of *"receiving* the Eucharist" confirms this reality. Receiving means believing in the One whom God has sent and, in our eucharistic experience, made available and accessible to us in this sacramental encounter.

Other passages in chapter six will offer us an occasion to consider the real presence of Christ in the Eucharist and how that presence summons us to faith. Before those considerations, however, it may be good to dwell on this primary dimension of eucharistic faith expressed in the words, *This is the work of God, that you believe in him whom he has sent.* Faith in the Eucharist is not primarily faith in the sacrament as such but in the *One whom God has sent* and who is truly present to us in the sacrament. This assent of faith, which may begin intellectually and affectively, marks the beginning of a path and a deepening process of connection and communion described in chapter six that will lead to the full interiorization and union with the One in whom we believe—*eat my flesh and drink my blood*—so that we share eternal life, the fullness of life, and even divine immortality—*they will have eternal life and I will raise them up on the last day.*

So they said to him, "**What sign are you going to give us then, so that we may see it and believe in you? What work are you performing?** Our ancestors ate the manna in the wilderness, as it is written, 'He gave them bread from heaven to eat.'" Then Jesus said to them, "Very truly, I tell you, it was not Moses who gave you the bread from heaven, but it is my Father who gives you the true bread from heaven. For the bread of God is that which comes down from heaven and gives life to the world." (John 6:30–33)

The two questions joined together in this passage—*What sign are you going to give us then, so that we may see it and believe in you? What work are you performing?*—are quite logical. The crowd accepts Jesus' words that to do the work of God means that they believe in the One whom God has sent. Understandably, they do not want to put their faith in Jesus as the One whom God has sent, unless they have some supporting evidence, so that their faith is reasonable and well-grounded. They then ask their question about a sign that Jesus might provide for them. Their second question suggests that the sign or assurance that they are looking for may be connected to the work that Jesus is performing.

Jesus' response initially appears to be very indirect with its reference to Moses, but on closer examination, he is very direct. There is no corroborating sign apart from the true Bread that God gives and that comes down from heaven, that is, Jesus himself. If at one time Moses interceded on behalf of a hungry people journeying through the desert and God sent manna from above to feed them, now there is no intercessor, only Jesus himself who is the Bread and gives life. The message is very clear. There is nothing outside of Jesus who is God's Bread come down from heaven to validate or corroborate the faith in him to which he summons people. In response to their question, Jesus gives no sign and offers no work. He is the sign. He is the life-giving Bread that is the work.

There is no sign besides Jesus himself. This conviction finds expression in other places in the New Testament. For example, when Paul writes to the Corinthians, he says, *"For Jews demand signs and Greeks desire wisdom, but we proclaim Christ crucified, a stumbling-block to Jews and foolishness to Gentiles, but to those who are called, both Jews and Greeks, Christ the power of God and the wisdom of God"* (1 Corinthians 1:22–24). Similarly, after Mark's account of the feeding of the four thousand, we read: *"The Pharisees came and began to argue with him, asking him for a sign from heaven, to test him. And he sighed deeply in his spirit and said, 'Why does this generation ask for a sign? Truly I tell you, no sign will be given to this generation'"* (Mark 8:11–12). There is no sign but Jesus himself.

Our eucharistic encounters with Jesus Christ are self-validating. We meet him who is God's Bread come down from heaven and who feeds us and who gives us life. There is nothing outside of this encounter to validate it or to substantiate it. The relationship itself is established by the sacramental presence of the Lord and our faith in him is the sufficient sign. The Eucharist is not a miracle, that is, a wondrous sign that points beyond itself to some heavenly or divine reality. Rather, the Eucharist itself is the encounter with heavenly and divine reality. For us who have met the Lord in the Eucharist, this is clear. We know when we encounter someone. We know when we have encountered the Lord who is our Bread of Life. The proof is in the meeting itself and in the relationship that comes alive and is expressed in the meeting.

> **The Eucharist is not a miracle, that is, a wondrous sign that points beyond itself to some heavenly or divine reality. Rather, the Eucharist itself is the encounter with heavenly and divine reality. For us who have met the Lord in the Eucharist, this is clear.**

They said to him, "Sir, give us this bread always." Jesus said to them, "I am the bread of life. Whoever comes to me will never be hungry, and whoever believes in me will never be thirsty. But I said to you that you have seen me and yet do not believe. Everything that the Father gives me will come to me, and anyone who comes to me I will never drive away; for I have come down from heaven, not to do my own will but the will of him who sent me. And this is the will of him who sent me, that I should lose nothing of all that he has given me, but raise it up on the last day. This is indeed the will of my Father, that all who see the Son and believe in him may have eternal life; and I will raise them up on the last day." (John 6:34–40)

Jesus moves the dialogue with the crowd forward. He directly declares that he is the Bread of Life and then unfolds the meaning of this identity. As the Bread of Life he not only sustains those who partake of him—*whoever comes to me will never be hungry, and whoever believes in me will never be thirsty*—he also saves them, that is, he saves them from sin and death and raises them to eternal life. Jesus is the Bread of Life in this sustaining and saving way as part of the Father's will and plan for all humanity—*this is indeed the will of my Father, that all who see the Son and believe in him may have eternal life.*

The implications for our eucharistic encounters with the Lord are astounding. When we meet the Lord in the Eucharist, we are face-to-face with the saving will of God that embraces us and all humanity. At the same time—and we must carefully note this—God does not impose his saving will on us. We must freely respond to his holy will and plan. Jesus says *whoever comes to me . . . whoever believes in me* can be embraced by God's saving will made present and active in Jesus Christ and manifested in his Eucharist. The mysterious interplay of divine grace and human freedom comes alive in the meeting of those who believe in Jesus present to them as the Bread of Life.

Then the Jews began to complain about him because he said, "I am
the bread that came down from heaven." They were saying, "**Is not
this Jesus, the son of Joseph, whose father and mother we
know? How can he now say, 'I have come down from heaven'**"?
Jesus answered them, "Do not complain among yourselves. No one
can come to me unless drawn by the Father who sent me; and I will
raise that person up on the last day. It is written in the prophets,
'And they shall all be taught by God.' Everyone who has heard and
learned from the father comes to me. Not that anyone has seen the
Father except the one who is from God; he has seen the Father. Very
truly, I tell you, whoever believes has eternal life." (John 6:41–47)

The dialogue of Jesus and his interlocutors moves into even deeper
realms of faith. Before, those who spoke with Jesus were identified
as "the crowd." Now they are named "the Jews." Perhaps they are
so designated to evoke another moment when God's people who
were in Exodus complained and when God fed them with bread
from heaven. *The whole congregation of the Israelites complained
against Moses and Aaron in the wilderness. The Israelites said to
them, "If only we had died by the hand of the Lord in the land of
Egypt, when we sat by the fleshpots and ate our fill of bread; for you
have brought us out into this wilderness to kill this whole assembly
with hunger." Then the Lord said to Moses, "I am going to rain bread
from heaven for you. . . . "* Moses then tells the people, *"Your complaining is not against us but against the Lord."* Then Moses said to
Aaron, *"Say to the whole congregation of the Israelites, 'Draw near to
the Lord, for he has heard your complaining'"* (Exodus 16:2b–3, 4a, 8–9).

The complaint in Exodus does not express a negligible disap-
pointment. Far more poignantly, it raises the question of whether
God will or will not save his people. Will he let them die in the desert? Similarly, the complaint of the Jews in dialogue with Jesus is
not about a marginally important disagreement that they have with
him. Their complaint goes to the heart of faith, belief in the
Incarnation of God's Son. Their question suggests their reluctance

to believe in Jesus as the One whom God has sent, the Bread that has come down from heaven: *Is not this Jesus, the son of Joseph, whose father and mother we know? How can he now say, "I have come down from heaven"?* Their experience of him and his human background seems to preclude anything divine about him. They have him figured out, as they might say. Precisely here, however, we encounter the mystery of the Incarnation, the Word made flesh. In ordinary humanity, the Word comes among us and dwells with us. That is the mystery of humanity and divinity in Jesus Christ.

Our encounter with the Eucharist links us directly with the mystery of the Incarnation. Do we not know who he is in his humanity? How can he say, "I have come down from heaven and am the bread of life"? This mystery and this invitation to faith intensify in the Eucharist: divine and glorious presence among us under the humble, common, and ordinary forms of bread and wine. Our eucharistic faith, once again, is clearly faith in the Son of God who has come among us. We profess our faith in the Creed and say: "For us men and for our salvation he came down from heaven, and by the Holy Spirit was incarnate of the Virgin Mary and became man." This Jesus professed in the Creed is the same Jesus whom we encounter in the Eucharist.

"I am the bread of life. Your ancestors ate the manna in the wilderness, and they died. This is the bread that comes down from heaven, so that one may eat of it and not die. I am the living bread that came down from heaven. Whoever eats of this bread will live forever; and the bread that I will give for the life of the world is my flesh." The Jews then disputed among themselves, saying, "**How can this man give us his flesh to eat?**" So Jesus said to them, "Very truly, I tell you, unless you eat the flesh of the Son of Man and drink his blood, you have no life in you. (John 6:48–53)

Jesus again identifies himself as the *bread of life*. This is no ordinary bread. It is *of life*, or as Saint Ignatius of Antioch (d. 110) in his letter to the Ephesians calls it "the medicine of immortality" (*pharmakon athanasias*). We will consider this dimension of the Eucharist when we reflect on verses 54–59. In this passage (verses 48–53), however, a new and important theme is introduced. It deserves our close attention.

Jesus says . . . *the bread that I will give for the life of the world is my flesh.* In response to this declaration the Jews raise the question, *How can this man give us his flesh to eat?* Both in Jesus' declaration and in the question of the Jews, we hear something about *giving.* Jesus says that the bread he gives for the life of the world is his flesh. His self-giving—it is his very flesh or self that he gives—as Bread will bring life to the world. Other places in the New Testament echo this self-giving or self-sacrificing action that brings life to the world. For example, we find this in Luke's rendition of the institution of the Eucharist at the Last Supper: *Then he took a loaf of bread, and when he had given thanks, he broke it and gave it to them saying, "This is my body, which is* **given** *for you . . . "* (Luke 22:19). Similarly, in an important passage in the Gospel of Mark, Jesus describes his mission or purpose and says: *"For the Son of Man came not to be served but to serve, and to* **give his life** *as a ransom for many"* (Mark 10:45). The self-giving of Jesus eucharistically or as the Bread of Life finds its foundation in his mission to give himself for us, so that we might live. The origin of this giving in the Eucharist and in the mission of Jesus culminating on the cross is to be found in God's love: *"For God so loved the world that he* **gave** *his only Son, so that everyone who believes in him may not perish but may have eternal life"* (John 3:16).

Our eucharistic encounters inevitably mean that Jesus is giving himself to us, and we in turn are receiving him. The full meaning of these eucharistic encounters emerges in a larger context. That larger context includes, in the first place, the love of God that prompts God to *give* the Son. The Son who has come down from heaven *gives* himself to us and for us definitively on the cross. The same Son as the Bread of Life *gives* himself to us sacramentally.

Human limitations force us to imagine steps or stages of giving. In fact, the giving is one, and it is God's self-gift and self-sacrifice in generative or life-giving love. Our contact with this giving is real and palpable in our meeting with Christ in the Eucharist, the one who is the Bread of Life. The giving, of course, is gift or sheer grace, nothing that we have earned, deserved, or merited. The receiving of the gift is in faith which accepts the word, the presence, and the life-giving self-sacrifice of Jesus, the Bread of Life, who comes to us in the Eucharist. Our eucharistic encounters distill the whole story of our salvation from God's gift of the Son, to the Son's self-sacrifice for us, to the availability of this gift in the Eucharist. What comes to us as gift then we must receive in faith. Again, we meet the mystery of God's grace and human freedom.

Now we can return to the question in the text—*"How can this man give us his flesh to eat?"* Jesus' listeners have taken his words, and now they frame them in a question that sounds like an impossible riddle. Like a Zen koan—for example, *What is the sound of one hand clapping?*—the impossible riddle-question about Jesus giving his flesh to eat is meant to push us into a new awareness or consciousness. Notice that Jesus does not answer their question. He does not tell them how he *can give* them his flesh to eat. He has already said that he *does give* them the bread that is his flesh for the life of the world. If he does it, there is no question about whether he can do it. Instead of responding to the question of how he can do this, Jesus simply insists, *"Very truly, I tell you, unless you eat the flesh of the Son of Man and drink his blood, you have no life in you."* The question of the people is about potential—*how can he?*—but the response of Jesus is about necessity—*unless you eat, you have no life in you.* The impossible riddle does push us into new awareness. If we had questions about the technical side of things, how he can do this, we recognize that in giving us the Bread of Life, he already does it. If we continue to question how it is possible, we come to know that we must leave that question aside to recognize that it is necessary for life itself.

Our eucharistic encounters tell us that only in union and communion with Jesus—eating his flesh and drinking his blood—can we truly have life within us. Everything else falls aside before that great reality.

The following verses describe that "life within us" that results from our union and communion with Jesus, the Bread of Life.

"Those who eat my flesh and drink my blood have eternal life, and I will raise them up on the last day; for my flesh is true food and my blood is true drink. Those who eat my flesh and drink my blood abide in me, and I in them. Just as the living Father sent me, and I live because of the Father, so whoever eats me will live because of me. This is the bread that came down from heaven, not like that which your ancestors ate, and they died. But the one who eats this bread will live forever." He said these things while he was teaching in the synagogue at Capernaum. (John 6:54–59)

We have heard a strong and uncompromising message in the words of Jesus. Unless we eat the Bread of Life which is his flesh for the life of the world, we have no life within us. Now in these verses he speaks of that life which dwells within us. The first descriptions of that life are that it is "eternal life" and it is life "raised up" on the last day at the end of time. It could seem that the life promised us is eternal—endless life as we know life now—or that it is life restored after death, but restored to what it was before death. In other words, initially it seems that the life promised is the life that we already have, only extended endlessly and restored if destroyed by death. In fact, a closer and fuller reading of the text leads us in a much different direction.

The eating and the drinking, we soon learn, are truly sacramental. They effect what they signify. The eating and drinking are a "taking within us" and amount to an internalization of the presence of the One who is the Bread of Life. We know that from text which reads: *"Those who eat my flesh and drink my blood abide in me, and*

I in them." In this verse is that favorite word of John, "abide" also translated as, "remain." It refers to mutual indwelling or presence within. We dwell in Jesus, and he dwells in us. Jesus then further specifies this by saying: *"Just as the living Father sent me, and I live because of the Father, so whoever eats me will live because of me."* Communion in the Body and Blood of Jesus draws us into the very communion of the Father and the Son. So, what are we to conclude from this about the exact meaning of the "life within us" that results from eating the flesh and drinking the blood of Jesus?

Clearly, the life within us because of sharing in the Bread of Life is not just an endless continuation of our current life nor is it simply restored life after death or at the end of time. These startling words of Jesus open an entirely new prospect for "life within us." In and through the Eucharist, "life within us" is already a sharing in God's own life. We are drawn into the very communion of the Father and the Son—*Just as I live because of the Father, so whoever eats me will live because of me*—a communion of the Father and the Son that is bonded by the Holy Spirit, who is their principle of unity and mutual love. This means that our eucharistic sharing draws us into the very inner life of the one God who is Father, Son, and Holy Spirit.

Our eucharistic participation already allows us to share in divine life, perhaps in ways that are mysterious and not fully manifest. Like a seed, however, that life buried within us is at work and will become evident as we make our great passage through death. So Jesus says, *"Very truly, I tell you, unless a grain of wheat falls into the earth and dies, it remains just a single grain; but if it dies, it bears much fruit"* (John 12:24). Again, in another place, in his dialogue with Martha, the sister of Lazarus, Jesus speaks of the enduring divine life within: *"I am the resurrection and the life. Those who believe in me, even though they die, will live . . . "* (John 11:25).

The Eucharist, we now realize, brings us life but not life as we have it, nor life as we know it. The life that the Bread of Life brings us is a participation in the very life of God, Father, Son, and Holy Spirit.

When many of his disciples heard it, they said, **"This teaching is difficult; who can accept it?"** But Jesus, being aware that his disciples were complaining about it, said to them, **"Does this offend you? Then what if you were to see the Son of Man ascending to where he was before?** It is the spirit that gives life; the flesh is useless. The words that I have spoken to you are spirit and life. But among you there are some who do not believe." For Jesus knew from the first who were the ones that did not believe, and who was the one that would betray him. And he said, "For this reason I have told you that no one can come to me unless it is granted by the Father." (John 6:60–65)

The question that the disciples raise is about the difficulty of Jesus' teaching. Because they have not fully understood his word or his teaching, they find it unacceptable. How, indeed, are we going to eat his flesh? Are we cannibals? What is this bizarre teaching that is so at odds with all our traditions of faith? These are, no doubt, the kinds of questions circulating in the minds and hearts of the disciples. These questions continue, because the disciples have not grasped Jesus' meaning. So, he reiterates his teaching in an unusual turn of phrase.

Jesus says: *"It is the spirit that gives life; the flesh is useless. The words that I have spoken to you are spirit and life."* And yet just a moment before, Jesus said: *"Unless you eat the flesh of the Son of Man and drink his blood, you have no life in you."* It does not seem in that context that "the flesh is useless." There, it seems to be the key to life. Here is the misapprehension of the disciples. Jesus is speaking of eating his flesh and drinking his blood as that Spirit-enabled mutual indwelling that opens to believers the very life of God within them. If it is only flesh apart from this life-giving relationship, then indeed it is useless. It makes no sense. There, in the life-giving and Spirit-enabled relationship, lies the meaning of Jesus' words: *"It is the spirit that gives life; the flesh is useless. The words I have spoken to you are spirit and life."*

This misapprehension of the disciples about "eating the flesh" of Jesus actually has a deeper source than their lack of understanding concerning the relational and spiritual dimensions implied by that phrase. The deeper source of this misapprehension is their fundamental failure to grasp in faith the reality of the Word made flesh, the Incarnation, the living Bread that has come down from heaven. That is why Jesus raises two questions of great importance: *Does this offend you?,* (or, more literally, *Does this scandalize you? Place a stumbling block in your way?*) and secondly, *Then what if you were to see the Son of Man ascending to where he was before?*

The second question—*what if you were to see the Son of Man ascending to where he was before?*—clearly speaks of the Incarnation. The question assumes that he has "come down," and so it echoes that most momentous verse of the prologue of John's account of the Gospel: *And the Word became flesh and lived among us.* (John 1:14a) Both the Incarnation and the Bread of Life are framed realistically with the word *flesh.* One can only understand Jesus' words about the Bread of Life as spirit and life, if they are grasped in faith in the Word made flesh, the Incarnation.

The second question—*Does this scandalize you? Place a stumbling block in your way?*—echoes other statements that see the Incarnation as a scandal or stumbling block on the way to faith. Faith in the Word made flesh is the fundamental foundation. So, when messengers from John the Baptist who is imprisoned come to Jesus and pose John's question to him—*Are you the one who is to come, or are we to wait for another?*—Jesus responds by giving signs of healing and preaching that belong to the Messiah and concludes by saying: *"And blessed is anyone who takes no offense [or, scandal] at me"* (see Luke 7:18–23). In another context, Paul speaks of the crucified Christ, the most dramatic manifestation of the word made flesh, as a stumbling-block or scandal (see 1 Corinthians 1:23). More positively and more constructively, according to the First Letter of John, the foundational criterion for all true faith is faith in the Incarnation: *By this you know the Spirit of God: every spirit that confesses that Jesus Christ has come in the flesh is from God, and every spirit that does not confess Jesus is not from God* (1 John 4:2–3a).

Our eucharistic encounters, we believe, put us in proximity to Jesus. They enable us to be close to him, indeed, to interiorize his very presence, so that he is our source of life and our being in communion with the Father, Son, and Holy Spirit. Prior, however, to our sense of coming close to Jesus Christ, is our faith that he has first come close to us, in coming among us as the Word made flesh who dwells among us. If this is our faith, we have overcome the scandal or stumbling block that would impede us from coming to him.

"But among you there are some who do not believe." For Jesus knew from the first who were the ones that did not believe, and who was the one that would betray him. And he said, "For this reason I have told you that no one can come to me unless it is granted by the Father." (John 6:64–65)

There is a sadness attached to Jesus' words—*But among you there are some who do not believe.* Unbelief is a reality for some and a possibility for all of us. God never imposes his gifts on us. We receive them, and we receive them in our freedom. That also means that we can refuse to receive what God gives us. As Jesus faces the unbelief of some among his disciples, he also summons us to engage our freedom in coming to believe in him, the Bread of Life.

Jesus also repeats a teaching that he offered earlier—*For this reason I have told you that no one can come to me unless it is granted by the Father.* Even our freedom is a gift of God. Graced freedom enables us to embrace the mystery of Jesus Christ, the Bread of Life.

As we stand before the Eucharist, we might do so recognizing that not only do we stand before the Bread of Life but also before the bread of freedom. When God rained down manna from heaven for his people, as we hear in the book of Exodus, he did so to enable them to continue their journey from slavery into freedom. Manna was a bread of freedom that enabled the Israelite people to go in Exodus. Jesus, who is the Bread that has come down from heaven, is also our bread of freedom. This bread sustains us on the journey from sin and death to new and eternal life. What comes from heaven is free or gratuitous. All we need do is receive it graciously and gratefully.

Because of this many of his disciples turned back and no longer went about with him. So Jesus asked the twelve, "**Do you also wish to go away?**" Simon Peter answered him, "**Lord, to whom can we go?** You have the words of eternal life. We have come to believe and know that you are the Holy One of God." (John 6:66–69)

In chapter six, Jesus is in dialogue with a more and more concentrated set of interlocutors. At first, there is a crowd, then his disciples, and now the Twelve. At each point, there is also an intensification of the questions and communications that pass between Jesus and his listeners. After not just a few but *many*, disciples no longer walk with Jesus, he turns to the Twelve and asks his question: *"Do you also wish to go away?"* And why would they wish to go away as the others did?

The claims and demands of Jesus have become more and more difficult to understand and to accept. He claimed to be the living Bread come down from heaven, which is his flesh for the life of the world. He demanded that whoever wanted a share of life must eat his flesh and drink his blood. Astonished at these words, and perhaps repulsed by them, but certainly unable to comprehend them, people walk away and leave his company. When Jesus turns to the Twelve, he knows that they have heard the same claims and demands that have pushed many of the disciples away. Surely, the Twelve were no more comprehending than the others who left, and they would have had no less difficulty in accepting his demands. *"Do you also wish to go away?"* Jesus says, but by implication he could just as well have asked, *"Why do you stay?"*

Peter's response with a question followed by an affirmation is very telling: *"Lord, to whom shall we go? You have the words of eternal life. We have come to believe and know that you are the Holy One of God."* In his answer to Jesus' question, Peter does not suggest that he has fully understood and accepted the claims and demands of Jesus. They may remain for him as difficult and challenging as they were for those who decided to walk away. Unlike those who walked away, however, Peter has discovered Jesus is not merely the bearer of a peculiar message or an imposer of difficult demands. Peter has discovered that Jesus speaks life-giving words and that his origins are manifestly in God. Whatever the difficulties of understanding Jesus' claims or acceding to his demands, Peter has discovered the person of Jesus behind the claims and demands. And that person of Jesus manifests the fullness of grace and truth. Will Peter stay? Yes, he will stay, because he cannot do otherwise, having met and discovered the one with whom he is staying.

When we encounter the Eucharist in a context of our own inexplicable losses, our own moral failures, or our incomprehension of the direction and hope of our lives, Jesus' question can press into us as it pressed into Peter: *"Do you also wish to go away?"* We may have very reasonable grounds for parting company with Jesus, at least from the perspective of our limited understanding. Still, we stay. We have not discovered a reason beyond Jesus, the Bread of Life, for staying with him. We have not discovered some confirmation or some comprehensible piece of evidence that makes sense of everything. Something else far more convincing has happened. We have met him alone and have come to know him. In knowing him, we have discovered his life-giving words and holy origins—all quite beyond our explanation but rendering us absolutely certain that there is no answer and no source besides him. Then we echo Peter's words: *"Lord, to whom can we go? You have the words of eternal life. We have come to believe and know that you are the Holy One of God."*

Jesus answered them, "**Did I not choose you, the twelve?** Yet one of you is a devil." He was speaking of Judas son of Simon Iscariot, for he, though one of the twelve, was going to betray him. (John 6:70–71)

Jesus has just addressed the Twelve and through his question—*"Do you also wish to go away?"*—called them to reaffirm their relationship with him. Peter spoke for the Twelve and said that they would stay with Jesus. When Jesus spoke to the Twelve and when Peter answered in their name, Judas Iscariot was included. Judas is included in this moment as he was included at the Last Supper, breaking the bread with Jesus and having his feet washed with the others. At these times, Judas seems—at least exteriorly—to be an integral part of the companions of Jesus, but he is not. Interiorly, he has split himself off from Jesus' followers. Interestingly, Jesus says of him, *"Yet one of you is a devil."* The word "devil" or *diabolos* literally means "one who splits off, cuts through, or separates." Judas is not the devil incarnate, but he does the devil's work, most especially in separating himself from Jesus and fracturing his own life.

Perhaps as we come to the end of chapter six of the Gospel according to John, we would like to have a more uplifting conclusion. We would like to leave this discourse on the Bread of Life with an inspiration or an illumination for our own encounters with the Bread of Life. Instead, we find ourselves face-to-face with the grim reality of Judas Iscariot and his betrayal. This is no accident in the text and in the teachings of Jesus.

It would be more convenient if the Gospel were to ignore Judas Iscariot or, at least, to minimize his presence as an unfortunate and regrettable sidebar in the story of Jesus. Consistently, however, the Gospel refuses to let us forget or minimize Judas. He certainly does not dominate nor define the story, but he is a clear and present figure. It is as if the Gospel does not want to let future generations of disciples forget this man who betrayed their Lord. And that is indeed the case, because his sad story serves a cautionary purpose for our own discipleship. Judas reminds us of our fragile hold on the saving mysteries of Jesus Christ. He reminds us of our pilgrim status—that we have not yet arrived at our full transformation and full participation in the life of God. He reminds us that we are quite capable of being inauthentic, that there could be a mismatch of our external behavior and the internal disposition of our hearts. He reminds us that we may be saved, but, as Saint Paul tells us, we are saved in hope (see Romans 8:24).

This last word given to Judas in chapter six may seem to strike a distressing or depressing note. I see it very differently. This word about Judas propels me more intensely into the eucharistic encounters that I have with Jesus, the Bread of Life. To know my fragility means knowing even more clearly Jesus' grace. To grapple with the horrible possibility of my betrayal tells me how dependent I am and must be on his grace. To see in Judas my own variance between exterior comportment and interior disposition of heart pushes me to steadfast discernment, never taking for granted that there is an even match of outside and inside.

No, in the context of my encounters with the Eucharist, the story of Judas is not fundamentally disheartening. It is certainly sobering. It compels me both to honesty with myself and to reliance on the Lord who alone can save me. In a most paradoxical way, in my eucharistic encounters, the story of Judas, who ultimately despaired, impels me to hope, because I learn to rely less and less on myself and more and more on the Holy One of God.

From the earliest years of the Church, commentators have noted that the Gospel according to John does not have a eucharistic institution narrative in the scene of the Last Supper. That absence has been explained variously, but regularly authors point to chapter six as the substitute for the institution narrative. There is, however, a portion of the Last Discourse of Jesus at the Last Supper that is very eucharistic. It belongs to chapter fifteen and it is Jesus' description of himself as the true vine. In my reading, chapter six and chapter fifteen's vine and branches illuminate each other.

> *"I am the true vine, and my Father is the vine-grower. He removes every branch in me that bears no fruit. Every branch that bears fruit he prunes to make it bear more fruit. You have already been cleansed by the word that I have spoken to you. Abide in me as I abide in you. Just as the branch cannot bear fruit by itself unless it abides in the vine, neither can you unless you abide in me. I am the vine, you are the branches. Those who abide in me and I in them bear much fruit, because apart from me you can do nothing."* (John 15:1–5)

From the vine comes the fruit that becomes the wine that becomes the Blood of the Son of Man, our true drink. Even before this process of transformation, while there is still the vine and branches, Jesus describes a eucharistic union that evokes the Bread of Life in chapter six.

Here in the vine and the branches, we come to understand the union of Jesus with those who believe. This is a living union of total intimacy; a union and not just a juxtaposition of vine and branches, but the union of both in a single, living organism. We who are the branches find ourselves in union not only with the vine but, in the vine, with other branches as well. The union grows and is dynamic, as it produces fruit. The union/communion glorifies God and moves to the completion of joy: *"My Father is glorified by this, that you bear much fruit and become my disciples. I have said these things to you so that my joy may be in you, and that your joy may be complete"* (John 15:8, 11).

Questions for Reflection and Sharing

1.   *This second section of the book considers chapter six of John's gospel and Jesus' presentation of himself as the Bread of Life. The whole section is meant to be a lectio divina, a slow and meditative reading of God's Word. Take some*

quiet time to read and sit with the entire chapter which can be found on pages 41–69. As you slowly reflect and pray on this chapter, what words, what images, what feelings surface for you?

2.   Place yourself in the crowd that was with Jesus. In other words, enter the scene of the gospel portrayed in John 6. What are you looking for from Jesus? What questions do you want to ask him? Do his words about the Bread of Life shake or challenge your faith? Do you draw hope from his words? Do you know more clearly and more deeply what he gives us in giving us the Eucharist?

3.   Remember that doing your own personal reflection and then sharing it with others will deepen and expand your understanding and appreciation of the text.

Chapter 4

What Does the
Eucharist Mean in Our Lives?

Introduction

At the very beginning of these reflections, I raised a question about the Eucharist. *What does the Eucharist mean? How does it matter?* Perhaps for some these questions raise further questions about doctrine. In fact, doctrinal concerns about the Eucharist are easily addressed. A consultation of the *Catechism of the Catholic Church* (1322–1419) yields a solidly informative synthesis of what Catholics believe about the Eucharist. For others, the question about the meaning of the Eucharist is a question about its history in the Christian tradition, how it has been received, celebrated, and even disputed. Again, resources are readily available to resolve questions of a historic nature. Finally, the question about the meaning of the Eucharist may take a more personal turn, and that kind of question requires particular attention.

If we ask about the meaning of the Eucharist in a personal context, we shift the question to an experiential range. In effect, we may be asking, "How does the Eucharist have an impact on my life? How does it enter into my experience and make a difference?"

Initially, it may seem that posing the question of the Eucharist in this way reduces the Eucharist to a subjective or even relative experience that may differ from individual to individual. In fact, that is not true. Of course, all spiritual experiences have a subjective dimension. Of their very nature, these experiences belong to individuals. At the same time, the Eucharist as the self-sacrificing and self-giving sacramental presence of the Lord in his Church has an objective value. It comes to us as gift before it is received subjectively into our particular lives.

> **If we ask about the meaning of the Eucharist in a personal context, we shift the question to an experiential range. In effect, we may be asking, "How does the Eucharist have an impact on my life? How does it enter into my experience and make a difference?"**

The question of the meaning of the Eucharist in this personal perspective belongs to the larger questions of spirituality that seek to identify, understand, and foster the subjective appropriation of the objective mystery of new life in Jesus Christ through the power of the Holy Spirit. We have already made important strides in answering this question of the meaning of the Eucharist, of how the mystery of the Eucharist enters into our experience and makes a transformative difference. Our initial step was to craft a eucharistic autobiography, to identify at least initially how across our lifetimes the Eucharist has indeed entered into our experience and changed our understanding, our affectivity, and our values. Although the sacrament is one just as the Holy Spirit is one, the spiritual experience of the sacrament is received into the unique experience of each individual. So, eucharistic autobiographies may share some common elements rooted in the one Bread of Life, but they will also always be unique narratives of grace.

Our second step was a careful examination of chapter six of the Gospel according to John, the Bread of Life discourse, paying particular attention to the questions in that chapter. In this discourse, Jesus explains himself as the Bread of Life and, even more, identifies how he wants to enter into the experience of his disciples in a transformative way. In other words, Jesus who is the Eucharist, an objective reality of faith, communicates how he wants to shape the subjective experience of his followers. In this happy conjunction of the objective and subjective reality of the Eucharist, we were able to find a deeper understanding of how the Eucharist enters and transforms our experience.

The third and final step will take some widely shared contemporary themes and concerns, in other words, shaping elements of human experience, and linking them with the Eucharist. In many respects, these themes are not just contemporary, since many before us have shared similar experiences. In their framing and in their urgency, these themes seem to belong to the questions of our time. They belong, if we can say this, to our collective subjectivity. And the Eucharist gives a direction and a shaping force to them. The question we ask is: *How can we link important elements of human and spiritual experience with the Eucharist?*

How can we link important elements of human and spiritual experience with the Eucharist?

The Eucharist and the Question of Life and Death

Here is a paradox. After our close reading of chapter six of the Gospel according to John, we clearly know that the Eucharist has to do with life. It is the Bread of Life. At the same time, the Eucharist immerses us into an experience of death. In the Mass, the eucharistic prayers, for example, frame the words of institution in the context of Jesus' Passion and Death: "At the time he was betrayed and entered willingly into his Passion, he took bread . . . "[1] Even more pointedly, Saint Paul says, *"For as often as you eat this bread and drink the cup, you proclaim the Lord's death until he comes"* (1 Corinthians 11:26).

Although we know that the Eucharist is the Bread of Life, we also know that it points us to the reality of death and that it also holds a promise of life beyond death: *"Those who eat my flesh and drink my blood have eternal life, and I will raise them up on the last day . . ."* (John 6:54). So, we can speak of the Eucharist in the context of life and death and eternal life. Perhaps we need to pause here, because we may be moving ahead of our experience.

Death in America is strange. Our American experience of dealing with death indicates that we are generally uneasy with our mortality. Our first line of defense against death is to deny it. It remains a largely unspoken reality, unless it glares at us in news accounts of wars, crimes, and natural disasters. When we plan for our future, rarely do we take death into account as a possibility. Another line of defense is to combat it at all costs. We combat it mainly through medical means. We are determined to eradicate cancer and heart disease. We mistakenly assume that with the right knowledge and technology, we can extend our lives indefinitely. Our final line of defense is to disguise it. When death happens as it inevitably does, we mask it with beautifully prepared corpses. And we even disguise death in funeral rites which more and more are called celebrations of life that incorporate eulogies that often take the form of a humorous roast of the deceased. There is something common in all these strategies of dealing with death. We cannot seem to allow ourselves to confront the grim reality of death as loss. We seem forbidden to grieve.

Even representations of an afterlife in popular literature do not strike a satisfying note. Think of Thornton Wilder's *Our Town*, Edgar Lee Masters' *Spoon River Anthology,* or the texts of bereavement cards that you can purchase at drug stores. Life after life seems like more of the same with the addition of some regret and perhaps a few sentimental flourishes. These conceptions of the afterlife are hardly inviting, nothing toward which you might want to move.

Biblical and faith descriptions of death and afterlife stand in stark contrast to the patterns of our popular culture. The biblical and faith traditions are, in my estimation, more real. They claim honest feelings of loss and sorrow. They are not sanitized, and they do not create illusions of immortality. They depict fear and anxiety as life draws to a close. They do not gloss over the harsh realities or the frightful feelings. In a paradoxical way, faith's honesty about death and its unflinching realism frees us from the illusion that we can save ourselves from dying. We cannot. And because we cannot, we must look elsewhere. That elsewhere is God who is the origin of life and life's destiny. Finally, faith speaks of afterlife, really, eternal life. Faith offers no detailed descriptions, a kind of travel brochure that we would like to have in hand as we depart from this world. Instead, faith tells us that we will be drawn into absolutely full life and absolute love. This afterlife is beyond our imagination but not beyond our hope, because we have come to know the One who makes the promise. This is Paul's message as he cites the prophet Isaiah: *"As it is written, 'What no eye has seen, nor ear heard, nor the human heart conceived, what God has prepared for those who love him'—these things God has revealed to us through the Spirit; . . . "* (1 Corinthians 2:9–10a).

The fundamental pattern of our lives in Christ is set at our Baptism and our faith-filled affirmation of Jesus Christ. Baptism provides the portal through which we enter a new existence in Christ. Permit me to cite Paul at length on Baptism. Then, we can link our Baptism with our participation in the Eucharist. Paul writes:

Do you not know that all of us who have been baptized into Christ Jesus were baptized into his death? Therefore we have been buried with him by baptism into death, so that, just as Christ was raised from the dead by the glory of the Father, so we too might walk in newness of life. For if we have been united with him in a death like his, we will certainly be united with him in a resurrection like his. We know that our old self was crucified with him so that the body of sin might be destroyed, and we might no longer be enslaved to sin. For whoever has died is freed from sin. But if we have died with Christ, we believe that we will also live with him. We know that Christ being raised from the dead, will never die again; death no longer has dominion over him. The death he died, he died to sin, once for all; but the life he lives, he lives to God. So you also must consider your-selves dead to sin and alive to God in Christ Jesus (Romans 6:3–11).

Our fundamental relationship with Jesus Christ forged in Baptism is union with him in his Death and Resurrection. His passage from life through Death to Resurrection is our passage as well, because we are one with him. Across a lifetime that union with Jesus in his Death and Resurrection is renewed and deepened in and through our participation in the Eucharist. At every step of our lives, we carry the consciousness of our dying and of our rising. The Eucharist itself fosters that consciousness and focuses our decisions for living, as we let go, for example, of an old way of living enslaved to sin, and as we embrace a new and free way of living. The Eucharist sustains the fundamental direction set by Baptism across our lives, until we come to the end. At that moment, we celebrate our personal liturgy of death and resurrection in union with him who is our life and Resurrection. We surrender into him who enables us to make the passage from this life through death to eternal life.

> **The Eucharist sustains the fundamental direction set by Baptism across our lives, until we come to the end.**

Inevitably, the question of death is or can become the central question of life for each of us and all of us. When death is not denied, combated, or sanitized, the question of death does belong to our culture and our time. Philosophers of the last two hundred years have alerted us to the question of death. Some, as Martin Heidegger, have identified human existence as *Sein-zum-Tode*, "being–toward-death," a reduction of who we are to pure contingency. Friedrich Nietzsche took another tack. In a world ruled by death, he extolled the "will to power," as a remedy for powerlessness, a remedy which easily led to nihilism and an ironic confirmation of the dominion of death.

Christian faith and, more particularly, eucharistic faith does not flinch from the reality of death. Death is embedded in the Eucharist, but so is life beyond death.

Questions for Reflection and Sharing

There are ten themes of human experience that are explored in this third part of the book in relationship to the Eucharist. They are: life and death; sexuality; God close to us and beyond us; violence; transformation; finding the moral measure of our lives; justice; our mission and purpose in life; human fragility; our future. These themes of human experience are powerful in shaping our fundamental attitudes toward life. They also raise challenging and important questions. After each section that presents a theme and its questions and its relationship to the Eucharist, consider the following questions for personal reflection and sharing with others:

1. Does the description of this particular human experience ring true to your own experience? If not, how would you frame or describe this human experience?

2. Do the questions triggered by each of these human experiences express the challenging dilemmas that we all face in the course of ordinary life?

3. From your personal perspective, how does the Eucharist cast light for you on the questions raised by important human experiences?

The Eucharist and the Question of Human Sexuality

The sexual revolution that blossomed in the 1960s promised greater freedom, deeper intimacy, truer equality between the sexes, healthier lives both psychologically and physically, and more fulfilling relationships. From those heady times to the present, sexual behaviors have indeed changed and become more casual, more short-term, more promiscuous, and riskier. The promises of sexual liberation, however, remain fundamentally unfulfilled. Large numbers of people find themselves at an impasse. The culture cannot imagine going back to a time of sexual repression or even moderation. At the same time, the current patterns are not fostering anything close to real freedom, intimacy, equality, health, and personal fulfillment. In the family of faith, however, there is some movement forward and some new paths that can break through the impasse.

In the early 1980s, Pope John Paul II offered a series of talks on the opening chapters of the Book of Genesis. He developed what was later called the theology of the body. With the biblical narrative of creation as a foundation and in a contemporary personalist framework, John Paul II began to lay a foundation for understanding human persons as sexual, but he did so in an integral context. How have we come to be who we are? What do our physical constitutions and the drives of our emotional lives tell us about an authentic life direction that we can embrace? How do the spiritual and physical come together in human beings who are both spiritual and physical? Is there something beyond us that gives us clues about our origins and our destiny? With questions such as these and with the biblical narrative and the traditions of faith, John Paul II began to detail a theology of the body that offered both understanding and direction for human sexuality.

> **How, then, does the Eucharist connect with human sexuality? In a word, both are about the body. Both are about the ways that we give our bodies.**

How, then, does the Eucharist connect with human sexuality? In a word, both are about the body. Both are about the ways that we give our bodies. Both are about ways of generating life. Both are about testaments of fidelity. Both point beyond themselves to the future.

First, we can consider the Eucharist in its dynamic of *giving*. An appropriate starting point might be the well-known words of Jesus to Nicodemus: *"For God so loved the world that he gave his only Son, so that everyone who believes in him may not perish but may have eternal life"* (John 3:16). Jesus brings us, if we can speak in an imaginative way, into the very heart of God. We find in Jesus' words an unqualified affirmation of God's love. It is a love so strong and so unflinching that it becomes self-giving. For in giving us his only Son, God truly gives himself. Indeed, in giving us the Son, he could give nothing more, because the Son is the full self-giving of God and God's fullest self-communication. See, for example, this passage from the Letter to the Hebrews: . . . *in these last days God has spoken to us by a Son, whom he appointed heir of all things, through whom he also created the worlds. He is the reflection of God's glory and the exact imprint of God's very being, and he sustains all things by his powerful word* (Hebrews 1:2–3a).

In the course of his ministry, Jesus often describes his mission or purpose with phrases such as "I have come to . . . " or "the Son of Man has come to. . . ." An important example of such a declaration of his mission occurs in the Gospel of Mark as Jesus defines the nature and scope of his service: *"For the Son of Man came not to be served but to serve, and to give his life a ransom for many"* (Mark 10:45). In this verse, Jesus connects this fundamental mission with his action of self-giving for the sake of the many who are ransomed or saved by that gift.

In the Gospel according to John, Jesus describes the same action of self-giving with the image of the Good Shepherd who freely lays down or gives his life for the sheep, so that they may have abundant life. Jesus says: *"The thief comes only to steal and kill and destroy. I came that they may have life, and have it abundantly. I am the good shepherd. The good shepherd lays down his life for the sheep. . . . For this reason the Father loves me, because I lay down my life in order to take it up again. No one takes it from me, but I lay it down, and I have power to take it up again"* (John 10:10–11, 17–18a).

Finally, Luke's rendition of the narrative of the institution of the Eucharist brings together Jesus' self-gift or self-sacrifice for our sake, the great action that is then memorialized or made present in the Eucharist: *Then he took a loaf of bread, and when he had given thanks, he broke it and gave it to them, saying, "This is my body, which is given for you. Do this in remembrance of me"* (Luke 22:19). Here, the giving of the bread, which is his body, is clearly emblematic of Jesus giving his life for us, that is, giving his body on the cross. In the Eucharist, all the elements that we have considered coalesce. The Eucharist makes present Jesus' self-giving, the giving of his body and life in generative and faithful love. From his sacrifice, we draw life and abide in God's everlasting love.

When we encounter the Eucharist, we meet the mystery of divine and enduring self-giving love that gives life. When we are in Holy Communion with that mystery, we draw its very power within us. Our lives are then being transformed into the image of Jesus Christ in his self-giving in generative and faithful love. Saint Paul says: *And all of us . . . are being transformed into the same image from one degree of glory to another . . .* (2 Corinthians 3:18). Through the power of Christ working within us by the Holy Spirit, our lives are directed, like his, to self-gift in generative and faithful love.

Recall that the self-giving of Jesus is literally embodied: *This is my body given up for you. This is my blood poured out for you.* And so for us, our self-giving is likewise embodied and enfleshed. Our self-gift, like that of Jesus, is not merely a matter of attitude or a spiritual disposition. It takes on bodily form. It means responding to the question: *What do I do with my body?* Those who have been joined eucharistically to Jesus respond by living as he did, that is, by giving over their bodies in generative and faithful love. Their living and their self-giving may be imperfect, but they have discovered a direction and a path given to them by their Savior.

The Eucharist summons us to decision and asks us: *What will I do with my body? How will I, like Jesus, give myself over?*

The Eucharist summons us to decision and asks us: *What will I do with my body? How will I, like Jesus, give myself over?* This eucharistic challenge affects the total direction of our lives, but in a particular way it confronts the direction that we will take with regard to our sexuality. The body, as we know from the two creation accounts in Genesis, is created as sexual: *. . . male and female he created them. God blessed them, and said to them, "Be fruitful and multiply . . . "* (Genesis 1:27–28). And in the second account, we find: *And the rib that the Lord God had taken from the man he made into a woman and brought her to the man. Then the man said, "This at last is bone of my bones and flesh of my flesh." Therefore a man leaves his father and his mother and clings to his wife, and they become one flesh* (Genesis 2:22–24).

Because of the effects of sin, sexuality left to its own devices devolves into lust, self-gratification, domination of others, or even a death-dealing destructive force. Sexuality drawn into the mystery of Jesus Christ's bodily self-giving in generative and faithful love finds direction and authenticity and, ultimately, a reclaiming of its holy purpose in the creator's design.

As we look to the Eucharist and as we look to ourselves, we ask, "What will I do with my body?" In that double perspective—both of the Eucharist and of ourselves—we begin to claim a direction and a purpose. Whether we are married, specially dedicated, or moving toward a given state of life, we find the essential elements of a response: "I will give myself over to God and to others. I will do so in ways that are life-giving. I will be in faithful communion with God and with others."

The specific questions of morality and the particulars of growth or development in the spiritual life belong to another set of reflections. Here, our concern is the Eucharist and the fundamental direction of our embodied lives. Here, our abiding question is "What will I do with my body?" Here, we take our cue from the brief but all-encompassing eucharistic words of Jesus: *This is my body given up for you.*

Both the Eucharist and human sexuality move toward the future. The Eucharist is pledge and promise of future glory. This is clear in the words of Jesus: *"Those who eat my flesh and drink my blood have eternal life, and I will raise them up on the last day"* (John 6:54). Similarly, Saint Paul links the Eucharist with the future glorious coming of Jesus Christ: *For as often as you eat this bread and drink this cup, you proclaim the Lord's death until he comes* (1 Corinthians 11:26). The eucharistic future is glory and full communion. Genuine sexuality, whether lived as a married person, a consecrated person, or a single person, is the energy that moves us ahead in ordinary life toward one day sharing in the fullness of life and communion with God and with one another. The Eucharist reminds us and empowers us to claim and live our sexuality authentically as self-gift in generative and faithful love.

Questions for Reflection and Sharing

See the questions on page 79 and apply them to this theme of human experience. Use the questions for personal reflection and sharing with others.

The Eucharist and the Question of God Close to Us and God Beyond Us

When I was pastor of Divine Savior parish, I instructed those who were going to serve as extraordinary ministers of the Eucharist. Of course, I needed to cover the rubrics or the official directives for distributing Holy Communion as well as some basic mechanics of the task. Even more importantly, I wanted to communicate the right frame of mind and spirit for those who would share with their brothers and sisters the Bread of Life. It seemed to me that people landed in two very different categories with regard to their attitudes about the Eucharist. One group took a rather casual, informal, and even friendly approach to the task distributing the Eucharist. They tended to smile at communicants and call them by name, if they knew them. If a host accidentally fell on the floor, they just picked it up without much break in their rhythm. The other group had a much different attitude toward the Eucharist. These people remembered a time when it was strictly forbidden to touch the Eucharist or even the sacred vessels that had held the Eucharist. They tended to be nervous about the task of distributing Holy Communion. Their demeanor was formal and, for some, quite stiff. If a host accidentally fell on the floor, they were very upset.

There is something right about both of these attitudes, and there is also something insufficient about each of them. I explained to the extraordinary ministers an important fact: *The Lord Jesus makes himself available and accessible to us in the Eucharist.* The simplicity of this statement belies its underlying depth and complexity. We can begin to understand it by reacquainting ourselves with the general sense of the sacraments. All the sacraments are effective signs of God's grace. All the sacraments make it possible for us to encounter the mystery of Christ across space and time. His Death and Resurrection and sending of the Spirit might seem locked in a given historical moment some two thousand years ago. The Lord who is seated at the right hand of the Father together with the Father sends the Holy Spirit upon the Church. Through that same Holy Spirit he makes the holy mysteries of his Death and Resurrection real and present in his sacraments and, preeminently, in the Eucharist. This means that the Lord Jesus Christ wants to come close to us, be available to us, and to be accessible in our lives and circumstances. This is the extraordinary power and wonder of the sacraments. Under simple and familiar signs, for example, bread and wine, Jesus and his saving mysteries are really and truly present to us, available to us, and accessible to us. God comes close to us and does so in familiar ways. The first group of eucharistic ministers seemed to understand this fact. It is not, however, the whole story.

The second group of eucharistic ministers understood another dimension of the sacraments, particularly, the Eucharist. It is not just any common presence made available to us in the sacraments and especially in the Eucharist. It is the *Lord Jesus Christ*. This is the incarnate Son of God. This is the Savior of the world. This is the very presence of divinity among us. Although there may be simplicity and familiarity in the sacramental signs, contained within them is the presence of the transcendent mystery of God made manifest in Jesus Christ. We are in the presence of the all-holy, the almighty, the all-merciful, light from light, begotten not made. We are creatures before our Creator, deeply limited people before infinite being, and sinners before the Holy One. And what ought to be the attitude before this transcendent mystery? It must necessarily be awe and reverence and even a holy fear.

I explained to the eucharistic ministers-in-training that they had a particular challenge. Their demeanor had to reflect the complex mystery of the Eucharist. It is a mystery of divine accessibility that enables us to come close to the Lord and his saving mysteries coupled with the reality of the holy and transcendent mystery of God. Neither stiffness nor chumminess will do. When we distribute Holy Communion, we stand in grateful familiarity with the Lord and loving reverence for the mystery among us.

This experience with the eucharistic ministers-in-training at Divine Savior refocused a larger sense of the Eucharist for me and even my appreciation for the mystery of God revealed to us. The

Scriptures speak of the immanence and transcendence of God, of God as close to us and God as infinitely beyond us. For example, in the Book of the prophet Isaiah, we find this affirmation of God's transcendent mystery: *For my thoughts are not your thoughts, nor are your ways my ways, says the* LORD. *For as the heavens are higher than the earth, so are my ways higher than your ways and my thoughts than your thoughts* (Isaiah 55:8–9). In the same book of the prophet, we find words that affirm an absolutely intimate and close relationship with God, a relationship that even surpasses the intimacy of mother and child: *But Zion said, "The* LORD *has forsaken me, my Lord has forgotten me." Can a woman forget her nursing child, or show no compassion for the child of her womb? Even these may forget, yet I will not forget you. See, I have inscribed you on the palms of my hands; your walls are continually before me* (Isaiah 49:14–16).

The prologue of the Gospel according to John captures the same mystery of divine transcendence and immanence manifested in the incarnation of the Word, God beyond us and God among us. The majestic beginning of the prologue proclaims the transcendence of the Word: *In the beginning was the Word, and the Word was with God, and the Word was God. He was in the beginning with God. All things came into being through him, and without him not one thing came into being. What has come into being in him was life, and the life was the light of all people* (John 1:1–4). Then, further on in the passage, the transcendent Word becomes a part of our familiar world: *And the Word became flesh and lived among us . . .* (John 1:14). That phrase "lived among us" is literally "pitched his tent among us." What we have discovered in the Eucharist finds not only a resonance but a foundation in John's prologue: God infinitely beyond us has come intimately close to us.

The doctrine of the sacraments and words of sacred scripture draw us deeper into the mystery of the Eucharist as the transcendent mystery come close to us in signs and terms that are completely familiar to us. We can find a further confirmation of this complex mystery and our complex experience of the mystery in the prayer experiences of great saints of our tradition. Saint Thérèse of Lisieux speaks of prayer in its transcendent aspect: "For me, prayer is an aspiration of the heart, it is a simple glance directed to heaven."[2] In this description, she echoes a traditional transcendent understanding of prayer as "lifting the mind and heart to God." The other Teresa, Saint Teresa of Avila, speaks of prayer in its immanent aspect: "For mental prayer in my opinion is nothing else than an intimate sharing between friends; it means taking time frequently to be alone with Him who we know loves us."[3] In her description of prayer, she echoes a traditional immanent understanding of prayer as "talking with God or dialogue."

We have moved through the practice of distributing Holy Communion to sacramental theology to sacred scripture to the saints of our mystical tradition. All this gives us a deeper appreciation of the complexity of our eucharistic experiences. It is great closeness and intimacy to be in the eucharistic presence of the Lord and to take him within ourselves in Holy Communion. It is a humbling and awe-inspiring experience to be in communion with the Lord of life in the Bread of Life. Besides our own appreciation of the eucharistic mystery, these insights may also help us to understand the puzzling contemporary question about the Eucharist. Why have people, at the rate of seventy-five percent, who have been initiated to the Eucharist chosen to withdraw from it or encounter it sporadically?

I do not have a precise answer to this question, but I do have some intuitions. In the current cultural climate, there is a process of social leveling that occurs. It manifests itself in the telemarketer who, without knowing you, addresses you by your first name. Ranking and hierarchies are suspect, and a kind of democratic familiarity with each other reigns supreme. Paradoxically, some in the culture do identify transcendent reality and forms of "spirituality" as desirable attainments, especially under the rubric of self-enhancement. Whatever is transcendent or spiritual, however, seems only accessible through exotic techniques usually imported from the East and hardly available to the general population. In other words, the spiritual and transcendent is quite removed. So, we have strong cultural bias toward relational familiarity—even when it is artificially constructed— coupled with a sense of tran-scendence that puts it outside of our ordinary and familiar ranges of life. If these currents of thought and attitude are present in today's cultural climate in the United States, then clearly it would be very difficult and probably impossible for many of our contemporaries to begin to understand and appreciate the Eucharist.

For our contemporaries, the Eucharist can be just a familiar symbol, something common and nothing special, certainly nothing you would genuflect before or nothing for which you would sacrifice extra sleep on a Sunday morning. Likewise for our contemporaries, whatever transcendence is to be had must entail some form of exotic and extraordinary personal journey. On the other hand, to have in the Eucharist the presence of the Lord, who remains transcendent and mysteriously beyond us but closely and intimately available to us—that does not compute. Either we are talking, they would say, about something close at hand or utterly beyond us. We in the family of faith, however, are affirming that in the Eucharist, it is both the transcendent and the immanent, the mystery that stays mystery but also comes close and enters our lives. Here, we may not have the answer to why people let go of the Eucharist. We may, however, have an analysis that identifies our key catechetical and communications challenge, if there is to be a eucharistic revitalization in the Church.

Questions for Reflection and Sharing

See the questions on page 79 and apply them to this theme of human experi-ence. Use the questions for personal reflection and sharing with others.

The Eucharist and the Question of Violence and Reconciliation

It is unexpected to link the Eucharist with violence. Our spontaneous images of the Eucharist suggest the peaceful realms of a congregation worshipping at Mass or the quiet of a chapel of adoration. How can the Eucharist be associated with violence?

Remember that the Eucharist is the sacrament of a sacrifice, the effective sign that makes present the sacrifice of Jesus Christ on the cross. Traditional language speaks of making that sacrifice present in an "unbloody manner." And, indeed, that one saving sacrifice of Jesus made present to us on the altar does not arrive in our worship with the sensory effects that were present on Calvary. There is no dust spattered with blood, no searing heat and accompanying thirst, no angry and mocking voices, no sound of nails being pounded, and no visible victim with a tortured body wracked by pain. In our Mass, we have the sacrifice and its heart in the self-giving of Jesus—*This is my body. This is my blood.* The enactment of Jesus' one sacrifice made present to us in a sacramental-liturgical action, however, must not let us forget the suffering and the violence of the sacrifice. Why is this so?

Clearly, our sense of the violence and suffering of Jesus in his self-sacrifice has nothing to do with a morbid spirituality that is drawn to dwell on gory details. Nor should a vivid recollection of this violence and suffering reduce our faith and relationship with the Lord to intense feelings of sympathetic distress, as I think some cinematographic representations of the Passion have done in recent years. No, the memory of violence associated with the sacrifice of Jesus is crucial, because it links us to essential elements of our redemption—the nature of sin and the heart of our reconciliation.

The effects of sin—from the very beginning in the Book of Genesis—are division and violence. As a consequence of sin, Adam and Eve are not only separated from God, they are also divided from each other: . . . *your desire shall be for your husband, and he shall rule over you* (Genesis 3:16). The story of Cain murdering his brother Abel reinforces the sense of sin as sundering the closest relationships of our lives and leading to violent destruction. The other chapters of proto-history in the Book of Genesis (through chapter eleven) chronicle the cascading effects of sin as division and violence.[4] Humanity seems endlessly and hopelessly caught in this cycle of division and violence breeding more division and violence. René Girard has convincingly demonstrated how only in Jesus Christ, who refuses to engage the retaliatory cycle of violence generating violence because of rivalry, do we find a breakthrough beyond the impasse of sin.[5]

On the cross and in his self-sacrifice, Jesus Christ absorbed within himself the power of sin, death, and violence, and then he destroyed it. The result is our great reconciliation with God and with each other. This is the teaching found in the Letter to the Ephesians:

But now in Christ Jesus you who once were far off have been brought near by the blood of Christ. For he is our peace; in his flesh he has made both groups into one and has broken down the dividing wall, that is, the hostility between us. He has abolished the law with its commandments and ordinances, so that he might create in himself one new humanity in place of the two, thus making peace, and might reconcile both groups to God in one body through the cross, thus putting to death that hostility through it (Ephesians 2:13–16).

The cross of Jesus and his sacrifice on Calvary represent a culminating point of violence and division that framed his entire earthly life. In the Gospel according to Matthew, the visit of the Magi to the newborn Jesus is accompanied by a violent threat to his life. An angel of the Lord appears to Joseph in a dream and says to him: *"Get up, take the child and his mother, and flee to Egypt, and remain there until I tell you; for Herod is about to search for the child to destroy him"* (Matthew 2:13). At the very beginning of his public ministry with his inaugural teaching in the synagogue of Nazareth, Jesus encounters fierce and violent opposition from his townsmen: *When they heard this, all in the synagogue were filled with rage. They got up, drove him out of the town, and led him to the brow of the hill on which their town was built, so that they might hurl him off the cliff* (Luke 4:28–29). The pervasive violence that marked the life and ministry of Jesus, a violence which culminated in the cross, alerts us both to our human condition and to the great gift of reconciliation and peacemaking memorialized and made present to us in the Eucharist.

In the New Testament, we find links between the Eucharist, the great sacrament of the sacrifice of reconciliation, and the raw human condition of division that can lead to violence. In Luke's account of the Last Supper, Jesus institutes the Eucharist and the Apostles partake of the bread that is his Body and the wine that is his Blood. This happens in Luke 22:19–20. Almost immediately after that and incomprehensibly from our perspective, we hear: *A dispute also arose among them as to which one of them was to be regarded as the greatest* (verse 24). It is a strong and difficult contrast, and we must assume that Luke has positioned it deliberately to make us confront the variance between our human and sinful inclination to division and the healing and reconciling work of Jesus manifested in the Eucharist. Similarly, Saint Paul writing to the Corinthians has instructed them on the reconciling power of the Eucharist when he says: *Because there is one bread, we who are many are one body, for we all partake of the one bread* (1 Corinthians 10:17). And very shortly, Paul speaks to the same community about its eucharistic inconsistency, that is, being divided even as they celebrate their unity and reconciliation in Christ: *For to begin with, when you come together as a church, I hear that there are divisions among you . . .* (1 Corinthians 11:18). He elaborates these divisions, especially those between the rich and the poor. Again, the juxtaposition of the great sacrament of unity/reconciliation with the all too human and sinful propensity to division invites us to consider our own depth of faith and our own willing commitment to enter into the mystery of reconciliation.

We have spoken of our "eucharistic encounters" as we participate in the Mass or as we pray before the Lord present to us in the Blessed Sacrament. These encounters lead us in various directions. A particularly significant direction has to do with division and violence and with reconciliation and unity.

When we meet the Lord in the Eucharist, we also meet ourselves and our world, which he has served and saved through his sacrifice on the cross. Although our eucharistic settings may be tranquil and undisturbed, we know that the Eucharist is the sacrament of a sacrifice. That costly sacrifice entailed a violent death which was itself the result of hostile divisions among people and a fundamental alienation from God. So, to meet the eucharistic Lord is to experience in our lives and in the world about us the divisions and the violence that take a daily toll on us. Far from removing us from the world and transporting us to some antiseptic realm, the Eucharist confronts us with the wounds and divisions of struggling humanity, including our own. In the sacrifice of Jesus present in the Eucharist, a sacrifice that entailed enduring violence, we are present to other victims of violence today and to the violence that we ourselves have endured.

Our eucharistic encounter with the sacrifice of Jesus does not leave us stalled in division and violence. Our meeting the Lord in his self-sacrificing love leads us to claim and share with him the victory of reconciliation and peacemaking. As members of his body and as those nourished by his Body and Blood, we come to recognize and to know that division, violence, and death do not have the last word. In the Eucharist, we recognize Christ our peace (see Ephesians 2:14). Our belief in him leads us to revise our prospects for all humanity. If the daily news fills us with stories of division, violence, and destruction, we can find ourselves in a very sorry state of discouragement. From the reconciling sacrifice of Jesus and our encounter with him in the Eucharist, we draw new hope and new vision for humanity. Healing, reconciliation, and unity are possible now in him who is our peace.

Finally, our eucharistic encounter with the peacemaking and reconciling sacrifice of Jesus empowers us to make a commitment to work in the Holy Spirit for the unity of all humanity.

Finally, our eucharistic encounter with the peacemaking and reconciling sacrifice of Jesus empowers us to make a commitment to work in the Holy Spirit for the unity of all humanity. The Eucharist then becomes for us more than a personal reminder of Christ's peacemaking, it enables us to embrace a path of living that brings his reconciliation to the whole world. Although this may initially sound grandiose, this mission and movement begins very simply in the context of our own lives, in our families, in our communities, and in the different worlds in which we walk.

Questions for Reflection and Sharing

See the questions on page 79 and apply them to this theme of human experience. Use the questions for personal reflection and sharing with others.

The Eucharist and the Question of Transformation

The town of Orvieto lies almost at the midpoint between Rome and Florence on a high hill. The cathedral, with its intricately ornamented façade, visually dominates the whole town. In a side chapel within the cathedral, frescoes by Luca Signorelli claim the attention of countless tourists and art lovers. Another chapel opposite the one with the Signorelli frescoes attracts those devoted to the Eucharist and eucharistic miracles. Housed in that chapel is the miraculous bleeding corporal of Bolsena.

A corporal is a small square piece of linen cloth much like a napkin. During the Mass it is unfolded and positioned in the center of the altar, and then the chalice and host are placed upon it. In a story, dating back to the year 1263, Father Peter of Prague, a priest from Bohemia, was making his way to Rome. He stopped in Bolsena, a town a few miles away from Orvieto, to celebrate Mass. The priest had doubts about the real presence of Jesus in the Eucharist. After the consecration, according to the story, the host bled onto the corporal, which then became an object of veneration and devotion.[6]

This miracle of the bleeding corporal of Bolsena is one among many miracle stories concerning the Eucharist. There is absolutely no obligation to believe these stories. They represent private or personal spiritual experiences and ought not to be confused with the public revelation that summons all of us to faith. I would offer two observations about these eucharistic miracles. I am skeptical of them as verifiable facts, because they seem to confuse the real sacramental presence of Jesus with his physical presence. These are two truly different kinds of presence. At the same time, I am convinced that these stories come from genuine faith and true devotion, and we need to pay attention to that far more than to the physical details of the stories. Devout people have often searched for answers to questions about Jesus present in the Eucharist. In the centuries surrounding the year 1000 AD, there were many questions about how Jesus was present in the Eucharist. Out of those theological and devotional circumstances came the various stories of eucharistic miracles.

Questions about how bread and wine become the Body and Blood of the Lord surfaced again in the context of the Protestant Reformation. In response, the Council of Trent proposed that the apt way to consider the change was contained in the term *transubstantiation*, that is, the substance of bread and wine really and truly become the substance of the Body and Blood of the Lord Jesus. What the Council of Trent proposed and what Catholic tradition has consistently taught as an article of faith to be held by all believers includes this basic conclusion: what was bread and wine is now the Body and Blood of the Lord.[7] Theologians and philosophers have also taken up the question of how it is possible that this can happen. That work of explanation is speculative, and, in my estimation, has not yielded any persuasive results. We have our faith that the change takes place, that Jesus is really and truly sacramentally present to us, and that this happens by the power of God through the invocation of the Holy Spirit and recitation of the words of institution by the priest in the Mass.

To my mind, Saint Cyril of Jerusalem (d. 386) expressed our faith in the change effected in the Eucharist with utmost clarity and precision and in a way that serves us well today. In the twenty-second mystagogical catechesis (teachings given to those who had been initiated into the Christian faith through Baptism and the other sacraments at Easter), Saint Cyril says:

> Since Christ himself has declared the bread to be his body, who can have any further doubt? Since he himself has said quite categorically, "This is my blood," who would dare to question it and say that it is not his blood? Therefore, it is with complete assurance that we receive the bread and wine as the body and blood of Christ. . . . Do

not, then, regard the eucharistic elements as ordinary bread and wine: they are in fact the body and blood of the Lord, as he himself declared. Whatever your senses may tell you, be strong in faith.[8]

Across the centuries both in theology and in devotion, much attention has been devoted to the change that makes bread and wine into the Body and Blood of the Lord Jesus Christ. Clearly, that attention is merited for such an important reality of faith. At the same time, limiting the focus to the change of substance has perhaps not enabled us to understand and appreciate the wider range of change and transformation associated with the Eucharist. We can consider that now, and then let it be a wider context for the change that we call transubstantiation.

To begin at the very beginning, the Eucharist encompasses change and transformation linked to God's creative power at work in nature. In the beginning, there is seed that grows and changes by God's providential care into wheat and into grapes. This growth and change happens silently and imperceptibly but inevitably by God's good care. This fundamental transformation is at the foundation of the Eucharist which requires wheat and grapes. Furthermore, this transformation already embodies the coming of the kingdom of God which the Eucharist celebrates. Jesus has shared this:

He also said, "The kingdom of God is as if someone would scatter seed on the ground, and would sleep and rise night and day, and the seed would sprout and grow, he does not know how. The earth produces of itself, first the stalk, then the head, then the full grain in the head. But when the grain is ripe, at once he goes in with his sickle, because the harvest has come." (Mark 4:26–29)

The change and transformation leading to and encompassing the Eucharist continues. Wheat and grapes become bread and wine. This does not simply happen. Human intelligence coupled with hard work yields this change that gives us bread and wine. The prayers of preparation of the liturgy describe this: "Blessed are you, Lord God of all creation, for through your goodness we have received the bread we offer you: fruit of the earth and work of human hands. . . . Blessed are you, Lord God of all creation, for through your goodness we have received the wine we offer you: fruit of the vine and work of human hands."

Human agency acts to transform wheat and grapes into bread and wine, but it is not human agency alone. God's providential care is at work in human activity, for we pray with gratitude for bread and wine received *"through your goodness."* In fact, God entrusts stewardship of the fruits of the earth to human beings from the very beginning and enables them to transform those fruits into food and drink. Shortly after their creation, God says to Adam and Eve: *"See, I have given you every plant yielding seed that is upon the face of the earth, and every tree with seed in its fruit; you shall have them for food"* (Genesis 1:29).

The transformation of seed into wheat and grapes and then, through human ingenuity and labor, their transformation into bread and wine are transformations leading to a eucharistic moment. When this bread and wine is brought to the altar and the Holy Spirit is invoked upon these gifts and the words of Jesus are spoken by the priest in the name and person of Jesus, they are transformed into his Body and Blood. "O Lord, we humbly implore you: by the same Spirit graciously make holy these gifts we have brought to you for consecration, that they may become the Body and Blood of your Son our Lord Jesus Christ, at whose command we celebrate these mysteries."[9] The Lord Jesus himself initiated this most holy transformation of simple elements of bread and wine into his Body and Blood. The most ancient account of the institution of the Eucharist is found in Saint Paul's first letter to the Corinthians. He gives strong testimony that he is faithfully handing on a tradition which he received ultimately from the Lord himself. He writes to the Corinthians and records the transforming eucharistic words of Jesus:

For I received from the Lord what I also handed on to you, that the Lord Jesus on the night when he was betrayed took a loaf of bread, and when he had given thanks, he broke it and said, "This is my body that is for you. Do this in remembrance of me." In the same way he took the cup also, after supper, saying, "This cup is the new covenant in my blood. Do this, as often as you drink it, in remembrance of me." For as often as you eat this bread and drink the cup, you proclaim the Lord's death until he comes (1 Corinthians 11:23–26).

If the growth of seed and the making of bread and wine signal transformations leading to the Eucharist, then there are other transformations that flow from and follow the Eucharist. By no means does transformation stop with transubstantiation.

When people receive the Body and Blood of the Lord in Holy Communion, they are changed and transformed by the grace and power of God. Recall the words of Jesus: *"Those who eat my flesh and drink my blood have eternal life, and I will raise them up on the last day . . . "* (John 6:54). What was weak and mortal, subject to death, is utterly transformed into the fullness of life, eternal life, and raised up on the last day. Only God can work this transformation, but God effects it as we receive the Body and Blood of Jesus Christ. Pope Saint Leo the Great spoke of this eucharistic transformation in this way: "For the effect of our sharing in the body and blood of Christ is to change us into what we receive. As we have died with him, and have been buried and raised to life with him, so we bear him within us, both in body and in spirit, in everything we do."[10]

The personal transformation effected by the Eucharist, although extraordinary in itself, does not exhaust the process of transformation. Believers who have taken within themselves the transforming Bread of Life are sent in mission to call the entire world to conversion and to transformation. That is the substance of the conclusion of Matthew's gospel, the "Great Commission": *Go therefore and make disciples of all nations, baptizing them in the name of the Father and of the Son and of the Holy Spirit, and teaching them to obey everything that I have commanded you* (Matthew 28:19–20a). This mission does not necessarily entail dramatic public actions or gestures. More likely, believers, who bear within themselves the transforming power of the Bread of Life, will themselves be a leaven that quietly, imperceptibly, but ineluctably changes the face of the earth. Jesus suggests this pattern in his parable of the yeast: *The kingdom of heaven is like yeast that a woman took and mixed in with three measures of flour until all of it was leavened* (Matthew 13:33). Saint Paul, too, seems to suggest this quiet but effective transforming presence and effect of Christians in communion with Jesus, when he writes to the Colossians: . . . *your life is hidden with Christ in God. When Christ who is your life is revealed, then you also will be revealed with him in glory* (Colossians 3:3–4). Finally, in the Sermon on the Mount, Jesus speaks to the transforming presence and effect of believers in the world, when he says: *You are the salt of the earth. . . . You are the light of the world* (Matthew 5:13, 14a).

What began as questions about transubstantiation, the change of the substance of bread and wine into the Body and Blood of the Lord, led us to a much larger horizon of change and transformation that has the Eucharist at its center. From seed comes wheat and grapes, which become bread and wine, which become the Body and Blood of the Lord, which become the principle of interior transformation for believers, who themselves are a leaven of transformation in the world. This is cascading transformation, elements of change linked and dynamically interconnected. Finally, we must affirm in faith that this cascading transformation moves to a final outcome. It is not simply change for change's sake. It is transformation that leads fully and entirely to God. Saint Paul communicates this vision when he writes to the Corinthians: *When all things are subject to him, then the Son himself will also be subjected to the one who put all things in subjection under him, so that God may be all in all* (1 Corinthians 15:28).

Questions for Reflection and Sharing

See the questions on page 79 and apply them to this theme of human experience. Use the questions for personal reflection and sharing with others.

The Eucharist and the Question of the Moral Treasure of Our Lives

The *Didache* or *The Teaching of the Twelve* dates to end of the first century. It provides one of the earliest witnesses to Eucharist in the life of the Church at its very beginnings.[11] The *Didache* contains a very challenging directive for the Christian community as it gathers to celebrate the Eucharist:

"On the Lord's day, when you have been gathered together, break bread and celebrate the Eucharist. But first confess your sins so that your offering may be pure. If anyone has a quarrel with his neighbor, that person should not join you until he has been reconciled. Your sacrifice must not be defiled. In this regard, the Lord has said: '"In every place and time offer me a pure sacrifice. I am a great king, says the Lord, and my name is great among the nations.'"[12]

The spiritual logic of this passage is clear. If Jesus reconciled us with God and with each other through his self-sacrifice on the cross and if his Eucharist makes that reconciling sacrifice present to us, then we cannot participate in the Eucharist unless we bring reconciled hearts to that celebration. The Eucharist becomes the moral measure of our lives. The more we grasp the full meaning of the Eucharist, the more clearly we recognize how we are to live. In the *Didache*, for example, the fundamental eucharistic reality of reconciliation summons us to reconcile with those from whom we have become estranged. There are, however, other dimensions of the Eucharist that give direction to how we live as the moral measure of our lives. We can reflect on some of these dimensions that give practical direction for our way of living.

Consider, for example, an absolutely fundamental direction for living—compassion. The Eucharist embodies God's compassion for his people. The Book of Exodus (see chapter sixteen) anticipates God's eucharistic compassion in feeding his hungry people with bread from heaven, manna. The Gospel accounts of the feeding of the multitudes not only anticipate the Eucharist which Jesus will give to his followers, but also the compassion which prompts him to bequeath that great gift. For example, Matthew's account of the feeding of the four thousand is quite explicit on this question of compassion: *Then Jesus called his disciples to him and said, "I have compassion for the crowd, because they have been with me now for three days and have nothing to eat; and I do not want to send them away hungry, for they might faint on the way"* (Matthew 15:32). The compassion of God in the Eucharist takes on another note, when we recognize the link between the Eucharist and Jesus' self-sacrifice on the cross. Saint Paul writes to the Romans: *But God proves his love for us in that while we were sinners Christ died for us* (Romans 5:8). In other words, the compassion of God manifested in the cross of Jesus and the Eucharist does not depend on the worthiness of those to whom God's compassion is extended. It is compassion without boundaries. It is compassion driven by love, not some meager form of pity for the unfortunate.

> **When we stand before the Eucharist and participate in it as the bread of compassion, we find a direction for our lives, a moral demand or imperative that ought to mark our interactions with others.**

When we stand before the Eucharist and participate in it as the bread of compassion, we find a direction for our lives, a moral demand or imperative that ought to mark our interactions with others. In other words, we receive the Eucharist and in the Eucharist, God's compassion. What we receive, we must give. We receive compassion, and we give compassion to others. And the compassion we give must be marked by those same qualities of the compassion we have received—genuine, driven by love, and without conditions placed on its recipients.

The Eucharist as the bread of wisdom and truth also gives us direction. Jesus says of himself that he is the truth. *I am the way, and the truth, and the life* (John 14:6). Saint Paul says of Jesus that he is *the wisdom of God* (1 Corinthians 1:24). Already in the wisdom literature of the Old Testament, we find the image of the bread of truth and wisdom. *Wisdom has built her house . . . she calls from the highest places in the town. . . . "Come, eat of my bread and drink of the wine I have mixed. Lay aside immaturity, and live and walk in the way of insight"* (Proverbs 9:1, 3–6).

Our engagement with the Eucharist—encountering Christ our truth and wisdom—forms us to be aware of deception and hypocrisy. This possibility for living in the truth may be the key to a passage in the Gospel according to Mark, which has often puzzled commentators.

Now the disciples had forgotten to bring any bread; and they had only one loaf with them in the boat. And he cautioned them, saying, "Watch out—beware of the yeast of the Pharisees and the yeast of Herod." They said to one another, "It is because we have no bread." And becoming aware of it, Jesus said to them, "Why are you talking about having no bread? Do you still not perceive or understand? Are your hearts hardened? Do you have eyes, and fail to see? Do you have ears, and fail to hear? And do you not remember? When I broke the five loaves for the five thousand, how many baskets full of pieces did you collect?" They said to him, "Twelve." And the seven for the four thousand, how many baskets full of broken pieces did you collect?" And they said to him, "Seven." Then he said to them, "Do you not yet understand?" (Mark 8:14–21).

An encounter with Jesus, the Bread of Life, stands in sharp contrast with the deceptive and manipulative *yeast of the Pharisees and the yeast of Herod*. Disciples, however, must understand who in truth gives the bread and who in truth is the Bread. Otherwise, they will fail to grasp the wisdom and truth of God. They will think, "We have no bread." Jesus, however, once truly encountered as the Bread of truth and wisdom enables his followers to see through the deceptive ploys and the foolish stratagems that surround them. He will enable them to live the truth in wisdom.

Because the Eucharist gives us Jesus Christ, the truth and the wisdom of God, this sacrament measures our lives. In and through the Eucharist, we will know what is untrue and foolish. And in a world so dependent on appearances and short-term results, this spiritual asset, which enables us to grasp what is truly real and to see all things according to their larger purpose in God's plan, is precious indeed.

The Eucharist is the moral measure of our lives in so many ways that these reflections can only begin to identify some of the possibilities. For now, we will explore one final dimension—the Eucharist and the path to justice. Consider justice in a large and expansive sense. Justice not only gives others what they are owed, although it certainly requires that. Justice, more largely considered, also means giving others what they need and doing so with an even-handed fairness and sense of equity. This sense of justice flows from a deep respect for the human beings who are a part of our lives whether they are closely connected to us or even if they are more distantly related to us throughout the world.

The feeding of the multitudes anticipates the Eucharist. Jesus feeds the crowds out of compassion for their hunger but also as a matter of justice owed people who have followed him and are now in need: *"I have compassion for the crowd, because they have been with me now for three days and have nothing to eat"* (Mark 8:2). Jesus' respect for the lives of those who have followed him moves him to a great work of compassion and justice in feeding them. In our own eucharistic encounters with the Lord, we come to feel his respect, compassion, and sense of justice in feeding us, his poor people. That pattern of justice—not only responding to what is owed but also to what is needed—shapes our own lives and our interactions with others.

The justice of Jesus evident in the Eucharist means fairness and equity in dealing with others. This is to be the pattern of our just living. A particularly challenging dimension of this fairness or non-partiality becomes clear in Saint Luke's account of the institution of the Eucharist: *Then he took a loaf of bread, and when he had given thanks, he broke it and gave it to them, saying, "This is my body, which is given for you. . . . This cup that is poured out for you is the new covenant in my blood. But see, the one who betrays me is with me, and his hand is on the table . . . "* (Luke 22:19–21). The phrase "his hand is on the table" haunts us as a reminder of the impartial justice of Jesus. Jesus has shared himself with his betrayer. Jesus has even-handedly fed all his disciples, including Judas, without regard for their worthiness. The Gospel according to John echoes Jesus' generous justice, when he washes the feet of all the disciples, including those of Judas (see John 13:1–30). Jesus feeds Judas and washes his feet, and we learn a new measure of living justly.

When we encounter the Eucharist, we meet the generous and even boundary-breaking justice of Jesus. Here, we find an extraordinarily challenging measure for our lives but also clarity of direction. This lived eucharistic justice echoes back to the voice of the prophets, for example, Isaiah, who spoke in God's name saying:

Is not this the fast that I choose: to loose the bonds of injustice, to undo the thongs of the yoke, to let the oppressed go free, and to break every yoke? Is it not to share your bread with the hungry, and bring the homeless poor into your house; when you see the naked, to cover them, and not to hide yourself from your own kin? . . . if you offer your food to the hungry and satisfy the needs of the afflicted, then your light shall rise in the darkness and your gloom be like the noonday (Isaiah 58:6–7, 10).

With these examples of reconciliation, compassion, wisdom, truth, and justice, we know the Eucharist as the moral measure of our lives, a direction for living as God wants us to live. Finally, we must be clear on how the Eucharist shapes us and forms us for living. In the Eucharist, the Lord does not issue orders that we are to live in this way or that. Our eucharistic formation happens not by decree but in an encounter with the living Christ. In and through the Eucharist we meet the One who reconciles, who is compassionate, who is wisdom and truth, and who works justice. We leave that meeting changed, reformed, and reshaped for living in a new way and, we continue to hold from that encounter a new way of measuring our lives.

Questions for Reflection and Sharing

See the questions on page 79 and apply them to this theme of human experience. Use the questions for personal reflection and sharing with others.

The Eucharist and the Question of Our Mission and Our Purpose

Elijah the Tishbite served as the great prophet upholding Israel's monotheistic faith in the face of great challenges. His mission was to maintain Israel's pure faith despite the infidelities of kings and people. And his mission was exhausting. Along the way, the Lord sustained him and enabled him to claim his responsibility and live his mission. When famine came to the land, the Lord provided for him: *The ravens brought him bread and meat in the morning, and bread and meat in the evening . . .* (1 Kings 17:6). Later, after he had slaughtered the priests of Baal, Elijah fled the relentless wrath of Jezebel, wife of King Ahab and promoter of false worship. The First Book of Kings gives this account:

(Elijah) went a day's journey into the wilderness, and came and sat down under a solitary broom tree. He asked that he might die. "It is enough; now, O LORD, take away my life, for I am no better than my ancestors." Then he lay down under the broom tree and fell asleep. Suddenly an angel touched him and said to him, "Get up and eat." He looked, and there at his head was a cake baked on hot stones, and a jar of water. He ate and drank, and lay down again. The angel of the LORD came a second time, touched him, and said, "Get up and eat, otherwise the journey will be too much for you." He got up, and ate and drank; then he went in the strength of that food for forty days and forty nights to Horeb the mount of God (1 Kings 19:4–8).

The Lord gives Elijah food. Notice, however, the food is not simply for his personal consumption or for the satisfaction of his own hunger. The food God gives Elijah is food for the mission, so that Elijah can assume his prophetic responsibility and continue the work entrusted to him by the Lord. Elijah receives food from God, so that he can give God's Word to the people of God.

The story of Elijah helps us to understand the Eucharist and mission in the New Testament. We can begin with the eucharistic stories of the multiplication of the loaves, especially in the Gospel accounts of Matthew, Mark, and Luke. Consistently, these accounts describe a very particular detail in the narrative. Jesus takes the loaves and blesses them and then *gave them to his disciples to set before the people* (Mark 6:41). Similarly, the feeding of the four thousand, Jesus takes the seven loaves *and after giving thanks he broke them and gave them to his disciples to distribute; and they distributed them to the crowd* (Mark 8:6).

Quite deliberately, Matthew, Mark, and Luke highlight a pattern: Jesus gives the bread to his disciples, so that they, in turn, may give it to others.[13] The bread entrusted to them means responsibility to continue the mission of Jesus in feeding the crowds. In its anticipation of the Eucharist, the story of the multiplication of the loaves identifies how we receive the Eucharist not only for our own sustenance—and that is certainly true—but beyond that as an empowerment and mobilization for mission. Our task and responsibility is to bring the one whom the Eucharist makes present to the entire world. Very simply, like the disciples in the Gospel, we receive the bread to give the bread.

Two other passages from Luke's writings underscore the relationship of the Eucharist to the mission entrusted to Christ's disciples. The well-known story of the two disciples on the way to Emmaus takes place in chapter twenty-four of the Gospel according to Luke (24:13–35). On their journey to the village of Emmaus, the two disciples try to piece together some meaning in the events that taken place in Jerusalem in the past week, events that led to the death of Jesus. In the course of their conversation, a stranger approaches them, explains the scriptures to them, and eventually stays to eat with them. We can directly cite the story from this point:

When he was at table with them, he took bread, blessed and broke it, and gave it to them. Then their eyes were opened, and they recognized him; and he vanished from their sight. They said to each other, "Were not our hearts burning within us while he was talking to us on the road, while he was opening the scriptures to us?" That same hour they got up and returned to Jerusalem; and they found the eleven and their companions gathered together. They were saying, "The Lord has risen indeed, and he has appeared to Simon!"

Then they told what had happened on the road, and how he had been made known to them in the breaking of the bread (24:30–35).

Notice this eucharistic moment—*he took bread, blessed and broke it, and gave it to them.* In the Eucharist, they recognize the Risen Jesus. Additionally, that experience of Eucharist mobilizes them to return to Jerusalem to share the good news with the other disciples—*that same hour they got up and returned to Jerusalem.* Their return to Jerusalem is not just a matter of temporal sequencing; first this happens, and then they go. The return to Jerusalem happens, because they have experienced the Eucharist with Jesus. The return to Jerusalem results from their empowerment and mobilization for mission.

Saint Luke, perhaps in a subtler way, locates the eucharistic foundation for responsibility and mobilization for mission in the Acts of the Apostles. At the end of chapter two of Acts, Luke provides a compressed portrait of the very earliest experience of the Church. He writes:

Awe came upon everyone, because many wonders and signs were being done by the apostles. All who believed were together and had all things in common; they would sell their possessions and goods and distribute the proceeds to all, as any had need. Day by day, as they spent much time together in the temple, they broke bread at home and ate their food with glad and generous hearts, praising God and having the goodwill of all the people. And day by day the Lord added to their number those who were being saved. (Acts 2:43–47)

As Saint Luke describes it, many elements of life emerge in the portrait of the early church in Jerusalem, including teaching, prayer, sharing of goods, and—of course—the breaking of bread, or the Eucharist. After the description of the internal life of the community, Saint Luke says: *And day by day the Lord added to their number those who were being saved* (2:47). In other words, the mission is taking hold, and more and more people are drawn into new life in Jesus Christ. It seems clear that there is a link between the internal life of the early church community with its center in the Eucharist and the effectiveness of its mission in outreach to and the incorporation of new people.

The dismissal rite at the end of the Mass clearly links participation in the Eucharist with the summons to claim responsibility and empowerment for mission. The words at the end of the Mass are clear. The celebration of the Eucharist is not a closed circle. Ultimately, the Eucharist mobilizes participants to do what Jesus wants them to do in the world, namely, to carry on and continue his mission. In that spirit, the deacon or priest can offer one of these formulas at the end of Mass: "Go forth, the Mass is ended;" or, "Go and announce the Gospel of the Lord;" or, "Go in peace, glorifying the Lord by your life;" or, "Go in peace." In the end, the relationship between the Eucharist and our mission is very simple. We give what we have received. And what we have received also enables us to share that with others. We are mobilized for mission and prepared to assume our responsibility for fulfilling God's purposes.

Questions for Reflection and Sharing

See the questions on page 79 and apply them to this theme of human experience. Use the questions for personal reflection and sharing with others.

The Eucharist and the Question of our Fragility

The first Eucharist was celebrated at the Last Supper. The Synoptic Gospel writers each give an account of that celebration. Although they differ in some details, the three accounts in the Gospel are in fundamental agreement. The narratives display a remarkable consistency in their portrayal of the Apostles who participate in the Last Supper. The portrait that emerges is not at all complimentary, a fact which suggests authenticity. After all, in the formation of the Gospel, one can conjecture that early leaders of the Church ought to look good. In fact, they do not. Gathered around the table with Jesus are the Apostles who share the Eucharist with Jesus. Very shortly, it will become evident that the Twelve includes one who will betray him, Judas Iscariot, one who will deny him three times, Simon Peter, and the rest—with the possible exception of John—who will abandon him out of fear.

The juxtaposition of the eucharistic sharing with the dismal behavior of Jesus' Apostles at the first Eucharist jars us and can leave us disillusioned. Our reflections on the Eucharist and Jesus as the Bread of Life have led us to grasp its power, beauty, and hope. Now, as we consider the Apostles at the Last Supper and what follows, we may conclude that we have idealized the reality of the Eucharist in our lives or perhaps have missed some major element of what it means to share the Eucharist. I think, in fact, none of this is true, but something of major importance is in play.

The Church and the Gospel clearly preserve a disturbing picture of the Apostles in relationship to the Eucharist at the Last Supper to instruct us today about our relationship to the Eucharist. Our life in Christ as his disciples is a fragile reality. As long as we are on the way, continuing the journey of our lives, no one of us can say that we have it cinched. We remain fallible, corruptible, in need of healing and transformation, until we draw our very last breath. Even our sharing in the Eucharist is no guarantee, not because of any deficiency in the Eucharist but because of the wounded hearts we bear as sinners. This humbling reality spurs us to an honest confrontation with ourselves. We need to look clearly and honestly at who we are, what we do, and what is our true purpose. Paul's words to the Corinthians about uncompromising self-reflection as they partake of the Eucharist make perfect sense in this context. This is not just a matter of making ourselves worthy to receive the Eucharist. We are never worthy. In fact, we say before our reception, "Lord, I am not worthy," and that is true. This self-reflection, as Paul describes it, serves to keep us from fooling ourselves, thinking that as long as we have our share in this sacrament all is well. We must know our fragile and wounded selves, in order to be faithful to this great sacrament. Paul writes:

Whoever, therefore, eats the bread or drinks the cup of the Lord in an unworthy manner will be answerable for the body and blood of the Lord. Examine yourselves, and only then eat of the bread and drink of the cup. For all who eat and drink without discerning the body, eat and drink judgment against themselves. For this reason many of you are weak and ill, and some have died. But if we judged ourselves, we would not be judged. But when we are judged by the Lord, we are disciplined so that we may not be condemned along with the world (1 Corinthians 11:27–32).

This knowledge of our fragility as we share in the Eucharist leads us to an ever greater dependence on God and an ever more complete surrender in trust into God's hands. Knowledge of our fragility, far from being a source of distress or even despair, pushes us more deeply to rely on the mercy of God. We become like the tax-collector of the parable, praying without ceasing, *"God, be merciful to me, a sinner!"* Then, we find our justification, not in our own merits but in the mercy of the One who holds us in all our fragility and brokenness and is able to heal us. And our sharing in the Eucharist is truer, not because we have overcome our fragility but because we have entrusted it to the One whose faithfulness is boundless.

In his great hymn to the Eucharist, *Lauda Sion*, Saint Thomas Aquinas describes the Eucharist as *cibus viatorum*, the "food of travelers" or, as we might also say, the "sustenance of pilgrims." The Eucharist accompanies those who are on the way, those who have not yet arrived, and those who are far from perfect in their love. In other words, it is the food of fragile people who ought not to trust in their own strength and who ought to recognize that they have not yet arrived at their destination. Perhaps, this is also the meaning of Paul's description of the Eucharist when he writes: *For as often as you eat this bread and drink the cup, you proclaim the Lord's death until he comes* (1 Corinthians 11:26). We celebrate the Eucharist often and over and over again. We do this waiting for Christ to come in glory. We also do this until we go to meet him in glory and finally find ourselves at home. In the meanwhile, we walk the way of pilgrims making progress, encountering obstacles, taking detours, failing to follow the proper route, correcting our direction, but always and in everything clinging to our hope in Christ Jesus.

Questions for Reflection and Sharing

See the questions on page 79 and apply them to this theme of human experience. Use the questions for personal reflection and sharing with others.

The Eucharist and the Question of Our Future

The context for our reflections has been the Eucharist as question. Surely, no question weighs upon us more than the question of our future. Fundamentally, we need hope that anticipates our future as much as we need food, water, and air to live. Without hope and a sense of the future, we are unable to live or to move forward. And so at a certain point the question of the Eucharist must join the question of the future. How is the Eucharist a key for both understanding and realizing our future?

A good starting point might be the prayer of Saint Thomas Aquinas, *O Sacrum Convivium,* "O Sacred Banquet." This brief prayer, which has been set to music in various well-known arrangements, identifies essential elements of our eucharistic faith. The text in Latin follows with an English translation.

O sacrum convivium,

in quo Christus sumitur;

recolitur memoria passionis eius:

mens impletur gratia:

et futurae gloriae nobis pignus datur.

O sacred banquet,

in which Christ is received;

the memory of his passion is renewed;

the mind is filled with grace,

and the pledge of future glory is given to us.

The last phrase of *O Sacrum Convivium* is truly haunting: ". . . the pledge of future glory is given to us." The Eucharist is not only the sacrament of the sacrifice of Jesus and the sacrament of his presence among us, it is also the great sacrament of our future glory. As the sacrament of our future glory, the Eucharist effectively makes present to us in an anticipatory way what is to be our heavenly destiny. In other words, in the Eucharist here and now we gain a glimpse of our future in the glory of God.

What do we glimpse in the Eucharist? In this sacrament which embodies the Death and Resurrection of the Lord, we see our full sharing in the fullness of Christ's risen life. We see our future and ourselves fully transformed. No longer do we partially share in the Lord's life, but we live in him, and he in us without qualification. Our future seen in the Eucharist is to *have life, and have it abundantly* (John 10:10b).

Even now the Eucharist we celebrate links us to the heavenly liturgy. Our worship is one with the eternal worship of Jesus Christ, the Son of God. *But when Christ had offered for all time a single sacrifice for sins, "he sat down at the right hand of God," and since then has been waiting "until his enemies would be made a footstool for his feet." For by a single offering he has perfected for all time those who are sanctified* (Hebrews 10:12–14). Our acclamation in our Eucharist celebrated on earth echoes the song of the heavenly seraphim in the innermost courts of heaven who day and night without ceasing, sing *"Holy, holy, holy, the Lord God the Almighty, who was and is and is to come"* (Revelation 4:8b; see Isaiah 6:3). Our future seen in the Eucharist is to *worship the Father in spirit and truth* (John 4:24).

Finally, our sharing in the Eucharist is a holy communion. Even now, we are being drawn into a sharing of the life of the most Holy Trinity: Father, Son, and Holy Spirit. And in our communion with God, we are in communion with one another. The essence of this communion is shared knowledge and mutual love, both beyond measure and beyond imagination. This sharing in Trinitarian life through word and sacrament begins now and finds its full realization in the vision of God. This is the message we hear in the First Letter of John:

We declare to you what was from the beginning, what we have heard, what we have seen with our eyes, what we have looked at and touched with our hands, concerning the word of life—this life was revealed, and we have seen it and testify to it, and declare to you the eternal life that was with the Father and was revealed to us—we declare to you what we have seen and heard so that you also may have fellowship with us; and truly our fellowship is with the Father and with his Son Jesus Christ (1 John 1:1–3).

Beloved, we are God's children now; what we will be has not yet been revealed. What we do know is this: when he is revealed, we will be like him, for we will see him as he is (1 John 3:2). Our future seen in the Eucharist is communion with the Father and the Son in the Holy Spirit, a sharing in the very life of God. That communion with God is foundation of our communion with one another.

At the end of the third eucharistic prayer of the Mass, the priest gives voice to the assembled community's great aspiration and hope that is sacramentally celebrated in the Eucharist: " . . . we hope to enjoy for ever the fullness of your glory." We can hold that hope securely. In the Eucharist, we have glimpsed the future. And it is a future of life fully transformed, of eternal worship that sings the praise and thanksgiving of God, and of full communion in the life of God and of our brothers and sisters in God.

Questions for Reflection and Sharing

See the questions on page 79 and apply them to this theme of human experience. Use the questions for personal reflection and sharing with others.

Part Three

Chapter 5

Conclusion:
Becoming the Body of Christ

The Eucharist is a question that takes many forms: What is its relevance or importance? What is the key to the meaning of the Eucharist? What are its effects or consequences? How does the Eucharist connect with deep human experiences and longings?

We explored the question of the Eucharist in various ways. We began by considering the question of the Eucharist in the Church today and how it seemed less central in the lives of those who claim to be believers. More than a question about individual believers, the initial question of the Eucharist took its bearing from the life of the Church community in today's historic moment.

Another turn of the question of the Eucharist took us in a related but different direction. The Eucharist, when it seems to have true power and meaning, decisively shapes our lives in a personal way. So, we explored the process of eucharistic autobiography, a trajectory of the Eucharist moving in and through our lives with its transforming power. Even here, in a context that is seemingly anchored in individual experience, the autobiography reveals a journey framed by community. In my own example of eucharistic autobiography, I found myself brought to the Eucharist by others, participating in it with others, or recognizing the implications that it held for me in living with others. For me and, I suspect, for everyone else, the eucharistic question unfolds in deeply personal ways but never in an exclusively private mode. This gift enters our lives and touches us not just one by one but together.

> **For me and, I suspect, for everyone else, the eucharistic question unfolds in deeply personal ways but never in an exclusively private mode. This gift enters our lives and touches us not just one by one but together.**

When we considered the Bread of Life discourse in chapter six of the Gospel of John, we discovered numerous important questions embedded in the text. All the dialogue concerning the Bread of Life hinges on the questions. The dialogue takes place between Jesus and an ever more sharply defined community. He converses first with the crowd, then the community identified as "the Jews," and, finally, with the disciples who have decided to remain with him, after others have walked away. The questions about the Bread of Life and the Eucharist intensify as Jesus engages those gathered before him.

The last set of reflections brought together questions about the Eucharist with significant questions about human experience. We considered nine questions that dealt with life and death, sexuality, the presence of God, violence and reconciliation, change and transformation, morality or living well, mission and purpose, fragility, and the future and hope. When coupled with the Eucharist, these themes or questions take on a spiritual or religious character. They are however by no means limited to specific faith commitments. In a true sense, these themes belong to the entire human family. They are universal human issues, and so they encompass people of every historic moment and culture. At the same time, the Eucharist, the sacramental presence of the Word made flesh, is situated in the middle of the human condition. In this way, the Eucharist raises questions and offers possibilities for the universal human concerns that we have taken up. In what it responds to and what it provides, the Eucharist embraces the whole human family.

After our reflections, it should be clear that the question of the Eucharist is not about a theological or religious concept that an individual might explore. The question of the Eucharist leads us to a deeper realm of shared identity. The Eucharist embodies the self-sacrificing presence of the One who is for us, *This is my body given up for you.* Consequently, the question of the Eucharist will inevitably bring us to the question of Christ for us in relationship to our lives lived for him. Ultimately, it is a question of shared identity: Who are we in him and who is he in us? The complexity of the question of the Eucharist derives from this dual dimension of identity which we can never forget.

> **The question of the Eucharist will inevitably bring us to the question of Christ for us in relationship to our lives lived for him. Ultimately, it is a question of shared identity: Who are we in him and who is he in us?**

Although we began with a pastoral question—the distressing situation of many believers drifting away from encountering the Lord in the Eucharist—the ultimate question is not about the Eucharist. The Eucharist remains forever the Bread of Life and the presence of the Lord. The Eucharist is forever the great sacrament of the sacrifice of Jesus Christ and the eternal worship that he offers the Father. The identity of the Eucharist is clear. The ultimate question may be that in drifting away from the Eucharist, have many people lost a sense of themselves in relationship to the very Lord of life?

The mysterious and inseparable conjunction of the eucharistic Body of Christ and the Mystical Body of Christ that is the Church— the *Christus totus,* the "whole Christ"—is a theme taken up by the Fathers of the Church. Their perspective argues for the conjunction of our eucharistic identity and our identity pure and simple as belonging to the Body of Christ. Their perspective leads us to see the question of the Eucharist as the question of our lives in Christ and Christ's life in us. Listen to three Fathers of the Church speak of this holy mystery.

From Saint John Chrysostom:

We must study this wonderful sacrament; we must learn the purpose of its institution and the effects which it produces. We are one
body, says the Scripture, and "members of His flesh and of His
bones." Let the initiated follow me.

He wishes that we become His body, not through charity
alone but that we be actually "mingled" with his own flesh. This
union is accomplished by means of the food which he has given us
as proof of His love for us. Therefore He has "mingled" Himself with
us, He has implanted His body in us, that we may be one, as a body
united with its head. What ardent love this manifests![1]

Similarly, Saint Cyril of Alexandria writes:

In His Wisdom and in accordance with the counsels of the Father,
the only-begotten Son has found a means of bringing and welding
us into unity with God and with one another, although by reason of
our souls and bodies we are each distinct personalities.

Through one body, which is His own, He blesses, by a mysterious communion, those who believe in Him and he makes them
concorporal with himself and with one another.

Who can now separate them or deprive them of their "physical" union? They have been bound together into unity with Christ
by means of His one holy body. For if we all eat of the one bread we
all become one body, since there can be no division in Christ. For
this reason is the Church called the body of Christ, and we severally
His members, according to the teaching of Saint Paul. Since we are
all united with the one Christ through His sacred body, and since
we all receive Him who is one and indivisible into our own bodies,
we ought to look upon our members as belonging to Him rather
than to ourselves.[2]

Finally, in his post-synodal apostolic exhortation *Sacramentum
caritatis*, "On the Eucharist as the Source and Summit of the Church's
Life and Mission," Pope Benedict XVI draws on three citations from
Saint Augustine:

The great Bishop of Hippo, speaking specifically of the eucharistic
mystery, stresses the fact that Christ assimilates us to himself: "The
bread you see on the altar, sanctified by the word of God, is the body
of Christ. In these signs, Christ the Lord willed to entrust to us his

body and the blood which he shed for the forgiveness of our sins. If you have received them properly, you yourselves are what you have received." Consequently, "not only have we become Christians, we have become Christ himself." We can thus contemplate God's mysterious work, which brings about a profound unity between ourselves and the Lord Jesus: "one should not believe that Christ is the head but not in the body; rather he is complete in the head and in the body."[3]

As we stand before the question of the Eucharist and the many ways that it unfolds, certain elements stand clear and will always be central to any response:

> *We receive the Body of Christ.*
> *We are the Body of Christ.*
> *We are becoming the Body of Christ.*

The beginning of this eucharistic identity is evident in the Gospels, when Jesus invites his disciples to draw life from him who is the Bread of Life. If we listen attentively to chapter six of the Gospel according to John, Jesus speaks not only about his Body that he will give as the Bread of Life, he is also forging the reality of the Church that will be his Body sustained by the Bread of Life. He proclaims himself as the Bread of Life and the necessity to eat his flesh and drink his blood in order to have life. He affirms that just as he has life because of the Father, so those who eat his flesh and drink his blood will have life because of him. He calls his listeners to faith. Many walk away from the invitation to believe. The core of his community of disciples stays, because they have discovered that he has the words of eternal life. They accept the Bread of Life and become the beginning of the Body of Christ in this world, his Church of which we are a part today. In this mysterious communion of identity, his and ours, we find a path of response to the question of the Eucharist.

Notes

Introduction: Eucharist as Question

1. Taken from the Office of Readings on the Feast of Saint Ephrem, June 9.

2. See: Albert Mirgeler, *Mutations of Western Christianity*, trans. Edward Quinn (London: Burns & Oates, Compass Books, 1964), pp. 44–65.

3. Council of Trent, DS 1642; see the *Catechism of the Catholic Church*, 1376.

4. See, for example, Charles Taylor, *A Secular Age* (Cambridge, MA: The Belknap Press of Harvard University Press, 2007).

5. *Lumen gentium,* 11.

6. *Presbyterorum ordinis,* 5. See: St. Thomas, *Summa Theol.* III, q. 65, a. 3, ad 1; q. 79, a. 1, c. et ad 1.

Chapter Two: The Question of the Eucharist in Chapter Six of the Gospel of John

1. The best summary of critical scholarship can be found in: Raymond E. Brown, S.S., *The Gospel according to John (i–xii)*, The Anchor Bible, vol. 29 (Garden City, N.Y.: Doubleday & Company, 1966), pp. 232–304. See also Rudolf Bultmann, *The Gospel of John: A Commentary,* trans. G. R. Beasley-Murray (Oxford: Basil Blackwell, 1971), pp. 209–237; C. H. Dodd, *The Interpretation of the Fourth Gospel* (Cambridge: At the University Press, 1968), pp. 333–345.

2. For example, in Mark 6:35–36: "When it grew late, his disciples came to him and said, 'This is a deserted place, and the hour is now very late; send them away so that they may go into the surrounding country and villages and buy something for themselves to eat.'"

Chapter Three: What Does the Eucharist Mean in Our Lives?

1. Taken from the second eucharistic prayer.

2. St. Thérèses of Lisieux, *Story of a Soul,* trans. John Clarke (Washington, D.C.: ICS Publications, 1976), p. 242.

3. St. Teresa of Avila, *Collected Works, Vol. I: The Book of Her Life,* trans. Kieran Kaanaugh and Otilio Rodriguez (Washington, D.C.: ICS Publications, 1987), p.96.

4. See Gerhard von Rad, *Genesis*. trans. John H. Marks (London: SCM Press, 1963), pp. 83–150.

5. See for example: René Girard. *Violence and the Sacred*, trans. Patrick Gregory (Baltimore, MD: Johns Hopkins University Press, 1977).

6. Joan Carrol Cruz, *Eucharistic Miracles* (Rockford, IL: Tan Books and Publishers, 1987), pp. 59–61.

7. The *Catechism of the Catholic Church* citing the Council of Trent offers this teaching: "The Council of Trent summarizes the Catholic faith by declaring: 'Because Christ our Redeemer said that it was truly his body that he was offering under the species of bread, it has always been the conviction of the Church of God, and this holy Council now declares again, that by the consecration of the bread and wine there takes place a change of the whole substance of the bread into the substance of the body of Christ our Lord and of the whole substance of the wine into the substance of his blood. This change the holy Catholic Church has fittingly and properly called transubstantiation.'" (1376).

8. Cyril of Jerusalem, *The Jerusalem Catecheses*, n. 22, as found in the Office of Readings for Saturday within the Octave of Easter.

9. From the third eucharistic prayer.

10. From a sermon by Saint Leo the Great found in the Office of Readings for Wednesday in the Second Week of Easter.

11. See Berthold Altaner, *Patrology*, trans. Hilda C. Graef, 2nd edition (New York: Herder and Herder, 1961), pp. 50–54.

12. See the Office of Readings for Wednesday of the Fourteenth Week in Ordinary Time.

13. I say that in the Synoptic Gospels there is a deliberateness about iden-tifying the process, because in John's account of the multiplication of the loaves, Jesus himself distributes the loaves. *Then Jesus took the loaves, and when he had given thanks, he distributed them to those who were seated . . .* (John 6:11).

Chapter 5: Conclusion: Becoming the Body of Christ

1. Saint John Chrysostom cited in: Emile Mersch, *The Whole Christ: The Historical Development of the Doctrine of the Mystical Body in Scripture and Tradition,* trans. John R. Kelly (Milwaukee: The Bruce Publishing Company, 1938), p 326.

2. *Ibid.,* p. 346.

3. *Sacramentum caritatis,* no. 36.